The Path of Initiation

Additional works in this series include:

The Nature of The Soul

Creative Thinking

The Soul and Its Instrument
(The Path of Initiation, Vol. III)

The Disciple and Economy

Leadership Training

Ashramic Projections

Healing
(Scheduled for publication in 2005)

Applied Wisdom
(Scheduled for publication in 2005)

These works are available through Wisdom
Impressions.

II

The Path of Initiation

Volumes I & II

By Lucille Cedercrans

Wisdom Impressions
Whittier, CA

The Path of Initiation

Volumes I & II

by Lucille Cedercrans

First edition, 2004

Wisdom Impressions is a group of practitioners of The Wisdom. Our purpose is to help create the appearance, support the teaching, and facilitate the distribution of The Wisdom.

Wisdom Impressions
P.O. Box 6457
Whittier, CA 90609-6457

The Great Invocation

From the point of Light within the Mind of God
Let light stream forth into the minds of men.
Let Light descend on Earth.

From the point of Love within the Heart of God
Let love stream forth into the hearts of men.
May Christ return to Earth.

From the center where the Will of God is known
Let purpose guide the little wills of men —
The purpose which the Masters know and serve.

From the center which we call the race of men
Let the Plan of Love and Light work out
And may it seal the door where evil dwells.

Let Light and Love and Power restore the Plan on Earth.

"The above Invocation or Prayer does not belong to any person or group but to all Humanity. The beauty and the strength of this Invocation lies in its simplicity, and in its expression of certain central truths which all men, innately and normally accept — the truth of the existence of a basic Intelligence to Whom we vaguely give the name of God; the truth that behind all outer seeming, the motivating power of the universe is Love; the truth that a great Individuality came to earth, called by Christians, the Christ, and embodied that love so that we could understand; the truth that both love and intelligence are effects of what is called the Will of God; and finally the self-evident truth that only through *humanity* itself can the Divine Plan work out."

Alice A. Bailey

Foreword

The following texts are the first two volumes of a three volume work known collectively as *"The Path of Initiation"*. Volumes I and II of this series first appeared in 1952 as *"Creative Thinking"* and *"The Nature of The Soul"*, respectively, while volume III appeared in 1956 as *"The Soul and Its Instrument"*.

However, in 1957, Lucille completely transformed the earlier texts (into the larger works we published in 2001 and 1993), but kept the earlier titles. Although the two sets of books are very different works, the duplicate titles were confusing, and it became customary to refer to the earlier versions as the "short forms" of C.T. and N.S.

In an effort to relieve this confusion, we have removed the earlier titles and are publishing the "short forms" simply as Volumes I and II of *The Path of Initiation*.

Students of these materials typically find volumes I & II very accessible, and excellent introductions to the basic principles of The Wisdom.

Sincerely,

Wisdom Impressions

August, 2004

Table of Contents

"In recognition of, and cooperation with this activity of the Soul, a *new thought-form presentation of The Wisdom* has been created and placed in availability for those who seek it. It can be contacted as an abstraction via the activity of meditation, and must then be translated into a concrete form by the one who meditates.

"This series of instructions is an interpretation of that new thought-form and has been written in an effort to aid man in the search for his Soul.

"For those who seek authority behind the written word, the truth of this text must be proven via its application. A formulated concept is of value only if it can be worked out as a living truth within the life and affairs of Humanity. Therefore do not look to the source of this teaching for its authenticity, but to the application of it within your own life and affairs."

The Nature of The Soul, pp. 3 - 4

The Path of Initiation

Volume I

The Path of Initiation, Vol. I

Introductory

Another Evolutionary Step

Basic Steps
Government, Laws,
Initiations
Group Consciousness

Man is taking another evolutionary step into a new kingdom, the Spiritual Kingdom of Souls. Already there are many who have taken the initial step. They are those who are consciously aware of themselves as Souls, and as such they work in the world to accomplish their purpose. They seek to aid man in his struggle to expand his consciousness of self, to consciousness of Soul.

This teaching is based upon the teachings of The Christ received from Him, via His messengers, as telepathic communication. It recognizes the Masters of the Wisdom as Emissaries of the One Master, the Christ. It is dedicated to serve with Them in the work of preparing race-mind consciousness for the appearance of The Christ.

The teaching is based upon certain basic concepts, which are briefly outlined as follows:

A. Government:

    1. That there is One Creator governing all creation.

2. That there is a group of Entities, headed by The Christ, who are The Creator's governing body for all evolving life in and on this particular planet. They do not at any time impose their will upon humanity, for man has been given the freedom of choice. They are, however, guiding humanity to its ultimate destination.

3. That there is a group of world workers who are aiding the former group, sometimes consciously, sometimes unconsciously, in their tremendous task. These individuals are highly evolved Souls, incarnating for this purpose. They are the enlightened, and sometimes the great men and women of the race.

B. Universal Laws:

1. The Law of Evolution. This is the Divine Law governing all creation, meaning that all consciousness is evolving upward, that all is a progress. God created Souls who are, as children, growing under the Law of Evolution to adulthood. The physical plane is but the school for this great cycle of evolving creation.

2. The Law of Reincarnation. This could be called God's grading system. The Soul incarnates not once in human form, but many times, growing in the school of experience to a higher state of consciousness. There is a misinterpretation anent this Law which must be corrected. Never does a human Soul incarnate in anything but a human body.

3. The Law of Karma or Retribution. This Law is the determining factor for the subject matter of any one grade. It is that which attracts to a man all that which is his own. If at one time he steals, at another time he will be stolen from, until he learns that it is not good to steal. If at one time he gives, at another time he will receive, so that he will learn that it is good to give.

C. Expansion of Consciousness:

1. That the physical form is but the vehicle of the Soul, and the personality is the instrument through which the Soul expresses itself.

2. That after the personality has evolved to a certain stage, a period of growth takes place in which the self-consciousness expands to include the Soul consciousness. This expansion covers five initiations.

These five initiations are:

a. The Birth of The Christ. In this stage the personality has discovered his Spiritual Soul, and has been born again in Christ Consciousness. Christ Consciousness is that higher state of being overshadowing humanity. It is That to which all men aspire. The initiation means, then, that the individual has finally discovered his True Self and the reason for his being. He lives, stands, and walks in the Light of The Christ, sharing that Light with all whom he contacts.

b. The Baptism. In this initiation the individual undergoes a purification process. Through disciplinary training, usually covering a period of several incarnations, his motives and desires become pure. As a result, his body is pure and he has gained control over his lower desire nature.

c. The Transfiguration or Illumination. This is the first major initiation, in which the consciousness becomes illumined, so to speak, with the Light of Truth. The individual undergoes a great awakening and begins, with Wisdom, to glimpse the cause back of all he sees. He is cognizant of the reality underlying all form manifestation and begins to think in terms of, and work with, energy.

d. The Crucifixion. The initiation in which the individual crucifies that part of his being which stands between himself and complete freedom. He sacrifices all personality ambition and desire to the One Life indwelling all form. He gives himself completely, works for, and is subservient to the One Life. After release from personal desire and ambition, he comes back to work in the world, but with one difference: his motive is love of Humanity, and all that he does is in service to his brothers.

e. The Ascension. This initiation is so advanced that very little can be said about it at this time. It is freedom from and mastery of the three planes of human endeavor—the physical plane, the astral plane, and the mental plane. The individual is released from the wheel of rebirth and if he does incarnate in human form, it is only in times of crisis for the guidance of humanity.

Man today is undergoing a difficult transition of which he knows little. He is completing the first initiation, and is approaching the second as a race—fluctuating between the emotional aspect of his nature and the mental. He is learning to react to life intelligently, rather than with just his emotions. As he becomes more and more polarized in the mental aspect, he comes closer to the revelation of his own Soul.

Still, man does have the freedom of choice, and should he decide to continue along his selfish path to destruction, he will undergo another period of dark ages in which the Spiritual Soul will be unrealized, and the completion of the first initiation still waiting.

There are some suggestions we would like to offer, as to the manner in which this series of instructions are studied. First, let us consider group consciousness, for that will eventuate as man comes into realization of his Soul, and tends to subordinate his personality to his Soul. Groups of individualities come into incarnation because of a long period of association which results in karmic relationships, and a certain aspect of the Divine Plan to work out together.

Those of you who are drawn to this teaching would do well to consider these relationships. All of those about you are Souls who are, in a peculiar manner, related to you and the working of the Plan. As you advance in realization, others will be drawn to you, and if you progress rightly, you and the others will enter into a group consciousness whose motive is Service, and whose goal is the manifestation of the Divine Plan, as you have grasped it, for humanity.

For this reason, we would suggest that those of you who are interested in the lessons, those who truly desire to aid man in the present crisis, and those who are geographically located so as to make it possible, study the lessons in group form. Meet however often as possible, or wise, and discuss the information contained in the lessons. You will find much greater progress can be made in this manner, and you will be amazed to discover how satisfying is group relationship.

A few words of warning can be interjected regarding groups; since you are functioning at this time as personalities, a certain amount of friction is bound to ensue, and unless carefully handled the group will not survive as such. Let Divine Love guide you in this enterprise. Recognize each as a Soul, and therefore your brother. Let tolerance be your attitude in all your relationships and give to each the freedom to express himself as he sees fit. Set yourselves not up as judges, but as brothers on equal footing, each striving to perfect himself in order to serve the many.

To those who are drawn to the lessons, but know not why, those who are curious, but doubting, we would advise to read and study, if so inclined, alone and with an open mind. Do not, as yet, try to enter into or form a group. Give others the right to believe and progress. When you are ready, then my brother, you will find your group.

Introductory

To all those who, through the universal Law of Attraction, are drawn to this teaching, we extend our sincere welcome. May ours be a long and joyous association.

The Path of Initiation, Vol. I

Lesson 1

The Path of Initiation

The Initial Step
Positive Thinking

This series of instruction is being written for all those who wish to enter into a study of metaphysics but have not sufficient knowledge of terminology and basic concepts to profit by such a study.

You will note that our title of the series has to do with the Path of Initiation; I should like to explain what is meant by that particular term in order for you to understand our realized goal and purpose of the presentation of this teaching.

In our introduction, we stated that the next evolutionary step for humanity is its entry into the Fifth Kingdom in nature, the Conscious Soul Incarnate. Man is differentiated from the animal by his ability to realize self-consciousness. The Conscious Soul Incarnate is differentiated from average man by his ability to realize Soul consciousness.

Initiation means a new beginning, in one sense, a birth. A path is the way of least resistance for the one who is traveling from one place to another.

The Path of Initiation is then the Path or Way of least

resistance for the birth of the Soul within the conscious awareness of man.

Our many series of lessons are designed to show man step by step the way into this new awareness.

The initial step upon the Path consists in right thinking, and so we have subtitled our first series, "Corrective Thinking."

Thought is the cause of all manifestation. A manifestation is the appearance of a material form, whether it be that of a child, a circumstance or situation, or a realized condition.

Each thought we think will take material form in our affairs eventually, depending upon the clarity and strength of that thought.

This may seem difficult to accept at first, for when you consider the many undesirable things that have happened to you, you wonder how you could have thought them into existence. To prove the truth of the statement, you only need to think back to those little everyday annoyances you constantly meet, and then remember how you think in regards to them. As an experiment do this:

> Consider something troublesome that is an almost everyday occurrence and then write down every thought you can remember thinking about it; as you catch yourself thinking about it at odd times, jot down those thoughts too. You will soon realize that where this subject is concerned, you are extremely negative in your thinking.

Lesson 1

Do not try to trace the big things, the really painful ones yet, for you are not ready to discover their cause. It lies buried in your subconscious and takes a different method of discovery.

After you feel you have pretty well dug up the negative thoughts in regard to this annoyance, deliberately counteract them with positive thinking. The first step is to stop feeling annoyance and meet the manifestation with interest. What is it trying to teach you? What lesson does it contain? Why have you considered it an annoyance in the first place?

The next and hardest step of all is to love it. Does this surprise you? Love is the Law of the Universe. It heals, soothes, and makes right. Nothing can stand against love, for love changes the character of that which we think of as bad to good. Out of bad will come good if it is met with love.

Then, regardless of how undesirable a thing is or even how evil it appears, learn to love it, and remember that one of the basic concepts of metaphysics is: There is no such thing as evil — it is only apparent evil and has behind it the purpose of God. "God works in mysterious ways His wonders to perform," and who can fathom His plan or call His manifestation's evil? Many may create apparent evil out of the error in his thinking, but even that is only apparent and done with the permission of God. God created man and gave him will. He gave him a right to exercise that will, knowing that sooner or later man would understand God's Will and It would become his own.

The last step is not so difficult after the second one has been taken. It just takes a little discipline. With love in your heart, replace the negative thoughts with positive ones. Write down all of the opposites to your negative thoughts and think them every time the subject comes to mind.

Lesson 2

Private World

Past Incarnations,
Idle Thoughts,
Happiness

In the first lesson we said that every thought will take material form eventually. In this lesson we shall go further and say that the little private world in which each one of us lives is but an outpicturing of what we have thought in former incarnations, have thought in the immediate past (that which lies behind in this incarnation), and that which we think now. In order to better understand this we shall now consider which of the three categories are responsible for various manifestations.

A. Past Incarnations:

If you have studied our introductory lesson, you realized that the human Soul incarnates many times, each time learning more of the Truth through experience, that Truth being added to its consciousness when again it takes a flesh body. Actually the incarnating entity creates in one incarnation the type of life it shall manifest in its next incarnation. It forms many associations and comes back again and again with those same people. It builds many dreams of what it would like to do, have, etc., and is unconsciously building the world into which it will return. When one stops to consider the quality of those dreams, it is easy to understand why we see so much suffering around us. How often do emotions of revenge, jealousy, hatred, greed, etc., color our dreams? When the incarnating entity fails to realize his dreams in one life, they will manifest for him in the next or the next, and if they are ugly thoughts, it stands to reason that the life in which they take form will be an ugly one.

These thoughts are the cause of the conditions into which we are born as children. They form the basis of our entire incarnation, for the first seven years of a child's life forms the patterns the rest of his life will take. All of the thoughts that are handicaps to healthy living are acquired in this age — that is to say, child-hood impressions which become complexes and block the healthy expression of the adult.

When you desire greatly something you cannot hope to have, you are building another life for yourself. You are actually creating future conditions into which you will be born.

B. Immediate Past:

When you think idle thoughts or passing thoughts, you are building the conditions into which you will move in a few years. Very often you will feel a strong desire for something, but it is replaced after a short time by a desire for something else. That which you desired, you are very likely to meet at a time when you realized you didn't really want or have need of it. Then you do not know what to do with it and it is a bother. Be careful when you desire something, making sure that it is not just a temporary whim.

Lesson 2

C. Present Thoughts:

Our present thoughts manifest the little things in our life that, when added up, tell the story of whether we are happy or unhappy. It is not the things which happen to us that cause our happiness, but rather our reactions to them. Happiness as a state of mind is possible of attainment under any condition. Life on the physical plane is never without apparent conflict, for conflict produces growth; but life anywhere can be pleasant. If we meet the challenge of life to the best of our ability, learn to accept the so-called bad with the good, and practice positive thinking, we are happy individuals.

Write a list of what constitutes positive thoughts and negative thoughts, and discover which ones you entertain most of the time. Check your list daily and see how many of the negative thoughts you can eliminate from your mind.

The Path of Initiation, Vol. I

Lesson 3

Where Thoughts Come From

The Mind and the Brain,
The quality of Consciousness,
The Environment

In this lesson, we are going to discover where thoughts come from. We know that we have a mind and a brain; but to most people, the mind and brain are something pretty vague and hard to understand.

The mind is a body of mental energy, interpenetrating every cell of the physical body; therefore, we call it the mental body. It is dual in nature, having two main functions and a third that evolves out of the two. The mental body is like a radio. It is a receiving and sending set capable of picking up electrical impulse, translating it into thought, and sending it out again to a desired destination. These two main functions, receiving and sending, can be combined in a way to cause the mind to be creative. All people are creative to a degree, but they are usually unconscious of the fact and have not fully developed their creative potential.

The brain is the instrument of the mind and the physical body. The mind impresses the brain with the thoughts it has picked up. The five senses, which have their mental counterparts, impress the brain with that which they pick up in the physical body and environment. The mind translates the impulse carried by the five senses into meaning and impresses the brain with that meaning.

It can be seen, then, that the brain does not think at all. It is an instrument of the mind and the personality consciousness. The mind impresses the brain with thought, and the personality consciousness absorbs the thought out of the brain.

The consciousness is the acting, thinking incarnating entity. It is that which interprets thought and utilizes it in its everyday living.

The quality of the consciousness is determined by its emotions, and the thoughts picked up by the mind are determined by that quality. A man who truly loves will pick up from the world of mind constructive thoughts of a high order, while the man who hates picks up destructive thoughts of a low order. The emotions, then, are the tuning device of the mind. They tune the mind into different frequency ranges of thought.

Actually, our consciousness lives in three worlds at once. It lives in the world of thought, in the world of emotion or of feeling, and in the world of physical plane activity. The world of emotion or feeling coordinates the world of the physical body, bringing the two together. Because of the emotions, thought takes material form.

We know now that what we feel determines the quality of thought we think. We also know that we are what we think.

Now to get back to our original intention in this lesson,

to discover where our thoughts come from. All about us are thoughts continually streaming by in the world of mind. They are the so-called good and bad thoughts, idle thoughts, constructive and destructive thoughts that people think all of the time. There are also thoughts in this world that have never been received by man and given material form. When the creative potentials are developed, man receives these thoughts and gives them material form. Thus, we have inventors, composers, authors, painters, etc.

A particular environment will manifest a certain type of condition according to the quality of its emotions. All of the people who make up the environment contribute to the general condition according to their emotions and thoughts. Man is a creature of habit, and tends to think what he has been influenced to think by those around him. He doesn't usually think for himself, but because he responds to the emotions of others, he picks up their thought and accepts them as his own. As he gives house within his own mind to these thoughts, they manifest in his life and affairs, and so he becomes a victim of circumstances.

If you want to change anything in your life, change your thinking about it. To do this, you must discover first what you are thinking, why you think it, and where it comes from. You would be surprised to discover how many thoughts flit momentarily into your mind that you aren't consciously aware of. They have become habits that are automatic and require no effort on your part. Take heed to your thoughts. Several times daily listen to your thinking.

When you discover what it is you are thinking, you may

be surprised and wonder why. Then is the time to look into your emotions. What has been your state of feeling? That is the why, remember, of what you have thought.

To discover where these thoughts come from, cast your mind into the environment. Look at the emotions of those about you, reflect back to their words, and realize what they are thinking. Is there a similarity in your emotions and thoughts to theirs? In this manner, you will discover if you are being unduly influenced in your thinking. It is also possible that your thoughts will be contradictory to others but, if the quality of emotion is characterized by resentment, etc., you will know you are still influenced because you are reacting.

In the next lesson, I will tell you how it is possible for you to be an influence for good in your environment. Until then, discover what you think, why you think it, and where the thought comes from.

Lesson 4

Brotherhood

Negative Thought,
Power for Good,
Become Positive to your Environment

By now, if you have followed the suggestions in Lesson 3, you realize that your environment exerts a very great influence upon you, and not all of it can be called good from your point of view. I doubt if you have considered anywhere near the entire environment that includes the radio, newspapers, community in which you live, etc., etc., and that is as it should be, for your immediate environment concerns only your sphere of influence. For instance, as you are influenced by others, so also do you influence them, and those who are most easily reached by you we say are within your sphere of influence.

What kind of influence do you wield upon others? Is it constructive? Is your influence a power for good? That, of course, will depend upon the way you react to others, whether you are positive or negative, and with what degree of determination or strength of will you exercise your influence.

Let us now consider what is meant by a negative thought. A negative thought is always one of denial. If you hate something, or someone, you are denying that thing or person the right to your love and so violating the basic relationship between you. The basic relationship between any two people is brotherhood, and is characterized by Love. Everyone has a Divine Right to your love, for all men are your brothers. It makes little difference how that relationship may manifest in the outer world. He may be your blood brother, a friend, husband, or even an enemy, but underneath the superficial relationship he is in truth your brother and has a right to your love. To deny that love is to break the universal Law of Relativity and bring imbalance into your life.

If you do not like a situation, you are denying your own growth. Within every situation is valuable lesson material for you. Remember, you have earned, in some way, everything that happens to you, be it pleasant or unpleasant. When a situation is unpleasant, realize that it contains within it a good lesson. Experience is the Great Teacher and one of God's laws. We experience that which we create. Learn then to love the situation for what it is, a lesson and grasp its Truth. As soon as you understand the lesson that undesirable experience holds for you, the situation will manifest no longer.

To become a power for good in your environment, you must become Positive to it. This means that it does not cause you to react negatively. You do not hate, resent, envy, fear, etc., but rather you love everyone and everything around you.

If you know someone who is full of resentment, how can you help that person? It cannot be done by becoming annoyed with his complaints, by agreeing with his resentment, or by avoiding or criticizing him. That is what is most commonly done.

Lesson 4

First, realize that within the heart of all men is good, and that recognition of, and concentration upon that good will call it forth. Look for and find the good within him, and then pour forth your love to him. Appeal with love to the good you know is there.

Then realize that within the mind of all men there is intelligence. The mind is, by nature, intelligent; if it appears differently that is because it has not been influenced to think intelligently. No one is by nature "dumb". In some cases the brain cells may have been damaged and in that case the mind is unable to impress the brain with intelligent thought, but in most cases it is simply a lack of right training that causes a person to appear below normal mentality. His mind has been influenced to pick up thoughts that are unintelligible or irrational, and his emotions have become perverted due to the denial of love by those around him. All cases of mental instability can be traced back to a great hunger for love.

To help this man, realize that he is, underneath all of the outer resentments, a child of God and therefore Good. Realize that he resents because he does not understand and because he hungers for someone to love him. Often he himself has so inhibited his own natural love that he does not know how, and he is hungering to love, as much as for it. Even though he does not understand, he is intelligent by nature and has the ability to understand.

Realizing all of this, bring the brother into your heart, loving him because he is your brother. At the same time, think towards him the understanding he needs to rise above his resentments. Do not speak to him until he indicates, through some action, that he is ready to listen to you. Hold your tongue and think. Then, if he asks your advice, give it.

Gradually, one by one, become positive to the conditions within your environment and give your help in the way described above where it is needed.

Lesson 5

Giving Advice

The Call to Service,
Judge Not,
Become Impersonal,
Planting Seeds

In our last lesson, I told you to give advice when asked for it. Today I wish to take this little matter of advice into greater consideration for it is very important. All of you who are led to read these lessons feel the urge within you to help others. That is part of evolution and characteristic of all who approach the Path of Initiation. The Soul is stirring within them, and they feel a desire to help others. This desire becomes so great as to be defined as a need. One of the characteristics of the Soul is service. Out of love for his brothers, and out of his compassion for them, he serves. It is this call to service that motivates most ministers, sincere teachers, many doctors, social workers, etc.

As the call to service becomes greater and greater, man finds himself hampered by his inability to help others. He may give them money, food, clothing, etc., but he knows that that is not the answer. There is something else, something he could give them that would really help. Then he begins to seek, to search for truth. This is true seeking, where man is motivated by a real desire to help others. This motivation will lead him unerringly to Truth.

I realize that often you become frustrated in the desire to help. You don't know how or what to do, and often make mistakes. One of the first ways in which the student learns to help is by giving advice, and this can be— if he is not very careful—where he makes his greatest mistake.

Before he is qualified to give advice, he must learn certain things and one of them is, "judge not lest ye be judged." He cannot decide what is right or wrong action for another person. He must not criticize or condemn— even silently—another for his actions, and therefore the only standard of right and wrong is for himself.

He cannot, then, consider even for a minute that something someone is doing, or has done, is wrong. He must realize that what the man is doing is right for him because that is where he is in understanding. He realizes that the things the man is doing will teach him needed lessons, and give him a full rich understanding.

Realizing these things, he then attempts to understand what it is the other doesn't realize. He sees, when he does not judge, what the man's next lesson is, and is then enabled to help him.

Another thing the student must realize before he can give the right kind of advice is that he must not impose his will upon another. He must not force his brother to accept that which he is not ready to accept. A refusal on the part of a brother to accept advice means that he is not ready to leave the experience behind. He must continue with it until he himself seeks a way out.

Lesson 5

The student of Truth then learns to hold his tongue until he is asked to speak. Even when the request is made, the student is very careful not to impose his will. He becomes impersonal and explains clearly, but without pressure, where the trouble is. His advice is in the nature of pointing out the way, in bringing the cause of the other's present difficulty into sight, and of bringing the way in which the difficulty can be overcome into sight. In other words, he brings the forked path into sharp focus, and the other is left free to choose the way he will go.

All the while he is doing this, he is pouring forth Love to his brother, realizing in the back of his mind the great healing power of Love.

After the brother has seen the forked path, and made his decision, the student must then abide by that decision. He does not say or think, "You are making a mistake." He knows the other is doing what he must do in order to grow, and that even if his words have not been sufficiently understood to immediately clear up the other's situation, he has nevertheless planted a seed that will in time grow and bear fruit.

I would speak a few words with you anent this planting of seeds, for that is what you are going to do when you give advice. To be sure your seeds will grow, you must know and recognize the planting season. You must know what is fertile ground, and you must help produce the conditions that are conducive to growth. The farmer sows his fields after they have been made ready by clearing and cultivation, and when the sun is in the right position to stimulate growth. Then, after the seeds are safely in the ground, he works with nature by giving them water and sometimes added food, and by continued cultivation.

The student of Truth must learn to do this if he is going to be of real help to others. He recognizes the season; that is, he responds to the other's indications that he wants help by preparing the ground for planting.

This preparation is the pouring forth of love and silent understanding spoken of earlier in the lesson.

When the other asks for help, the student plants his seed: a realization of the forked path.

After the planting, he aids nature by his continued projection of love and silent understanding, plus pulling the weeds as they grow with the seed planted.

This subject of pulling weeds we shall take up in our next lesson. In the meantime, think more about planting seeds, about what constitutes productive ground, and how it can best be prepared for sowing.

Lesson 6

The Spring of Consciousness

The Seeds of Truth,
Recognizing Weeds,
Pulling Weeds at the Right Time,
Divine Will and Divine Love

Today we are going to learn how to pull weeds. It is a law of nature that good ground will produce both that which is planted, and that which is latent within the ground itself.

So it is with man. Latent within him are the "weeds", those undesirables which have been acquired through years and centuries of living. The common names for some of these weeds are:

Fear	Greed
Jealousy	Criticism
Resentment	Prejudice
Pride	Intolerance

Many of these weeds have not as yet had a chance to grow due to lack of nourishment. Certain conditions are necessary to stimulate growth of any kind, and man, like all other forms of nature, goes through cycles or seasons. Many individuals are passing through the winter of their cyclic activity. In other words, they are at an apparent standstill insofar as the growth of their consciousness is concerned. In a sense their consciousness is sleeping. The body is automatically performing the functions necessary to daily living, but the incarnating entity is apparently making no expansions of understanding.

Then comes the spring and the consciousness stirs with new life. It looks about with newly opened eyes, observing its activities and the activities of others with greater interest. It stirs, and awakens to the One Life indwelling all form, and begins to grow. Like the flower, it lifts up its head into the light of the sun, and rises above the earth. This does not, of course, mean that man literally moves from earth, but rather, that his attention is turned from that which is material to that which is spiritual.

As he does this, he suddenly receives new energies, spiritual energies, which stimulate the growth of his consciousness. Into his mind and emotions are planted the seeds of Truth, and they take root and grow. The vital life energies, which are pouring through him from his own Soul, feed and nourish that which has been planted and is desirable, as well as that which is latent within him and is undesirable. The negativity he has acquired springs up as a bed of weeds along with the positive concepts of Truth. Thus it is that we often see a man, who has taken a step forward upon the Path into a newer and broader understanding, develop some characteristic which is undesirable and becomes an obstacle in his path to further progress. Very often such a one becomes critical, criticizing and judging those who do not think as he does. Sometimes he develops pride and thinks of his growth as an accomplishment which places him just a little above others. These are the weeds which must be eliminated if the plants are to ever bear fruit.

The first step in learning how to do this is to realize that these weeds are there and will grow, and must be pulled. No man is exempt from this process, though many do not recognize it. Therefore, if you feel that this does not apply to you, better look again, for a weed is escaping your vision.

The second step is to learn not to be dismayed when you discover a weed. It is a good sign for your ground is fertile and your garden growing.

The third step is to discover and to eliminate the weed at the right time. It must be large enough for you to see, in other words, making itself obvious either in your attitude or activities, and not too deep rooted for you to pull. Do not let a weed grow too long; neither attempt to pull it before it is obvious. If you let it grow too long, its roots will be so deep that in pulling, you will break them off, leaving some to grow again. If you attempt to pull a weed to soon, you may pull the wrong thing and so eliminate a rootling of that which you have planted. Be sure then that your weed is obvious before you attempt to eliminate it from your garden. However, once it is obvious, and you know it to be a weed, waste no time; pull it.

The last step is in the pulling of the weed, and that is very important. As you pull something, pressure is applied in a pulling manner from above, and as it comes out it is revealed in its entirety.

Your garden tools in this instance are Divine Love and Divine Will. First you realize that you are the gardener, the Divine Soul, and that you can do anything you wish with your garden. You can let it become a bed of weeds or a wonderful garden of spiritual food for the spiritually hungry.

Then you bring your will to bear upon the weed. Your will is your intent, and is actually the plan of your garden. You see it as you wish it, in your own mind, and then follow through with Divine Love.

Divine Love is a wonderful tool, and can be used in many ways. One of its characteristics is its quality of magnetic attraction. The steady application of Divine Love, impulsed by Divine Will or intent, will gradually draw your weed right out of the depth of your garden, and into the light of day where it can be seen, roots and all. Then you will know its cause, and the weed will have been instrumental in the growth of your understanding.

Let your application of Divine Will and Divine Love be so gentle so as not to break the weed, and steady so as to assure its elimination.

First, you must learn to do this yourself in your own garden; later you will be able to help others. You can begin helping others by pulling your own weeds, and becoming a radiating center of love and light to them.

Lesson 7

The Effect of Sound

The Dominant Note,
The Sound of Your Voice

In this lesson, we are going to consider the effect of Sound upon the world in which we live. Sound plays an important part in your life, influencing you in ways of which you are but dimly aware.

Sound sets into motion the substance of which all forms are made. It may increase, decrease, or even change direction of the already existent motion of the substance, but it always has its effect, and that effect has to do with its vibratory frequency.

All substance has motion; the speed of its motion is defined as its frequency, and manifests as sound.

We know, then, that every particle of substance, within and without our bodies, is moving at a definite frequency, and is sounding its own peculiar note. The aggregate of these notes within a form (such as the human body) emits a peculiar dominant note which is the key vibration of that particular organism.

The dominant note or vibration can be seen in manifestation in the tonal quality of the voice, in the quality of the emotions, and in the response the individual makes to his environment. Thus, when one speaks, he betrays to the one who knows, the degree of harmony or discord he is bringing into manifestation. When each particle of substance has been brought into right relationship with each other particle and the central directing Life (the Soul), then the sound produced is in complete harmony and can be likened unto the music of the spheres.

All new sound has its effect upon all existent sound, and can be consciously directed to create a desired condition. It is easy to see how the sound of a voice will effect the sound of the particles of substance within a body, either increasing or decreasing this frequency, and creating a condition of harmony or discord. A kind word, for instance, spoken at the right time, and carrying the right tonal quality, can soothe troubled emotions, and bring harmony into a condition of discord. It can do even more; it can bring a feeling of well-being to one who is ill, and if spoken by one who knows, it can heal.

Stop for a moment, and think of all the different sounds which reach you every day. The sound of the voices of all those people with whom you come in contact, the radio, the planes flying overhead, the automobiles in the street, the electrical appliances in your home, the animals, the birds, the wind; all of these and many more are making themselves known to you via sound— and that sound has its effect upon you and your environment—but most of all you are influenced by the sound of your own voice.

Go back to the sound of your voice just prior to receiving this lesson. What was its tonal quality? What impressions was it making upon you and others? What type of influence was it exerting? Was it positive or negative? How do you feel as you remember it?

Now speak your name slowly, and carefully, allowing your voice to pitch itself. Analyze the tonal quality. Is it soft, low, high, scratchy, harsh, purposeful, controlled? This is extremely important, for it will tell you the degree of harmony you have established within yourself. If its tonal quality is melodious and beautiful without any attempt on your part to make it that way, then you have developed a fine degree of harmony between the three aspects of your nature: the mental, emotional, and physical.

If it is unsteady and inclined to rise in pitch at the end of a word, this means you are divided within, that the mind and emotions are not agreed as to purpose, and decision is then difficult for you to reach.

If it is too loud, this indicates that you are self-centered, superior, and very insecure emotionally.

If it is too soft and indistinct, the indication is that you are torn by imaginary fears, that you worry and fret over nonessentials, and that buried deep within your subconscious is a guilt complex.

If it is harsh or scratchy, it indicates that you have not adjusted to your environment, that you do not accept your responsibilities, and that you are driven by buried hostility.

These are but a few of the examples of what the voice reveals. Listen to your voice as you speak to others, and as you go about the process of daily living, and analyze it. See if you can discover the environmental areas with which you have not established harmony or right relationship. In this manner you will be preparing yourself for the information in the next lesson which will concern itself with how you can utilize sound to bring harmony into your life and affairs.

Lesson 8

Sound

Tuning the Mind,
A Condition of Peace

In our last lesson, we discussed the tonal quality of the voice, and how it reveals the degree of harmony or discord the individual is manifesting.

We also considered sound and the general effect it has upon substance. We mentioned the fact that sound can be consciously utilized to create a desired condition, but we did not go into detail about this.

In this lesson I shall go into detail on this subject and not only entertain a concept which is new to most of you, but learn how to put it to practical use in your daily life and affairs.

Consider first the effect of music upon our modern civilization. Many individuals have the preconceived idea that music evolves out of our present culture, but this is not so. Music, as a whole, is one of the instruments which produce a culture, and which molds a civilization into certain patterns.

You will remember that back in lesson three I told you that the mind has a dual function which, when utilized in a certain manner, gives it a third function. The mind is a receiving and sending set. When the emotions are used to tune the mind in on the right frequency, it is used to pick up thoughts which have not been given concrete form by the world of men. These thoughts lie out of reach of average human experience and are called abstractions. When man is able to tune in on them and receive them he clothes them in concrete mind substance, and gives them form. Thus an abstraction becomes a beautiful piece of music, or literature, or a beautiful painting, etc. This is the creative function of the mind which is that third function arising out of the ability to receive thought and reproject it. In this case it is projected, as creative art, onto the physical plane. Thus a thought-form is materialized as a physical form.

These abstractions which creative artists bring down as music, art, literature, inventions, etc., play an important part in the building of civilization. They steer humanity (so to speak) into certain types of experience which are felt by all men.

Music has its effect primarily upon the emotions of the race. It brings them an emotional awareness of relationships which they would be unable to reach without it. For instance, the man who cannot sing, play music, or compose it, can still reach the feeling tone of certain relationships by hearing music. A young couple always have what they call their "tune" or "song", and this is because that particular piece of music crystallized in their feelings of which they were only partially aware. It is no accident that so many young people realize that they are in love while dancing to a particular melody, or while hearing it on the radio, etc.

The man who sings, while he possibly cannot compose

music, can reach that feeling tone the composer knew, by singing it; so we see that the composer actually brings an abstraction down into concrete form for others to know. He is serving the race, sometimes without even realizing that he does so.

Listen to different kinds of music and analyze its effect upon you, paying particular attention to that which you have not heard before. What type of experience is it designed to produce? What effect does it have upon the masses who hear it?

Then realize that in the same manner in which the composer received the abstraction and gave it concrete form, you too can utilize sound to create a desired condition in your environment.

First, decide upon the effect you wish to create and why. Are you motivated by selfish desire or out of a desire to help another? If you wish to bring a condition of peace to the troubled emotions of someone close to you, and you are sure it is being done out of a real desire to help them, then do the following:

1. Think of the individual with love and understanding. Take him into your heart and feel the peace you would have him know.

2. Then with your mind, reach out to God for the right words to say to him, or the right thoughts to send him.

3. When you feel you have them, speak them, or think them, and on a wave of Love sent toward him, speak aloud the words, "So Be It."

Try this for a while without any physical contact with the brother you are helping. Whenever you speak about him, do so with the thought of the help you are giving, and the feeling of Love you have for him, and then watch the tonal quality of your voice. You will note a definite change in it, and that change will have its effect upon the condition.

Peace be with you.

Lesson 9

Speech

Realizing Brotherhood,
The Effects of Words,
The OM

We shall continue our study of sound, considering today one of its forms of manifestation, that of speech.

Speech is a very important tool of man, in that it allows him to communicate his thoughts and feelings to others. Via communication certain relationships are established and evolved until eventually the relationship of brotherhood is realized.

Speech plays another very important part in a man's life which he seldom recognizes, though the world is more aware of the power of words than ever before. Speech is a tool which can be used to bring about manifestation. It crystallizes a thought and feeling into concrete form by setting up a vibration in physical plane substance which attracts it into manifestation.

While speech evolves as a result of a state of consciousness, and is therefore an effect, it nevertheless becomes in turn a cause and brings about an evolution of consciousness as its effect.

For instance, let us consider man when his state of

consciousness was such that the concept of want was first realized. He experienced a sense of lack, of need, and coined a sound which was the equivalent of our word "want". Let us say he wanted food. He was aware of hunger, was discontented as a result and sought food. Eventually his seeking brought him food and satisfaction. He was no longer aware of lack.

After many repetitions of this experience, man became aware of another want: a need for a mate. He sought her out, and went on to new wants until eventually, many centuries later, man stood on the threshold of a new age experiencing a new want, one for his Soul. He needed to fill himself with the Love of God, and so his want became something new, an aspiration. The state of consciousness which had coined the word want, had expanded and grown by the experience it had produced, until the consciousness was such that it no longer thought in terms of want. It aspired to God.

Students of metaphysics are taught to guard their speech, and speak only after careful thought, for words have a way of producing the very effects one may not desire.

As an example, if a man declares over and over, "I am so poor, I want more money;" he is creating the poverty in which he lives, by his words. How could it be otherwise; he states emphatically, "I am so poor. I want more money." All of nature contrives to bring his exact words into manifestation.

The words, "I am," are an assertion of your authority in the world in which you live. We have already seen that we create that world with our thoughts and emotions.

Lesson 9

When we say, "I am," we are asserting our mastery here, and whatever follows those two words is a proclamation that will surely come into being. Thus to say, "I am poor," or "I am sick," insures the continued manifestation of your poverty or your illness. Such is the Law.

In man's efforts to shape sounds which will more clearly describe his thoughts, many languages have evolved. He uses many words to describe the shaded difference of his thought or feeling, the tonal quality of a feeling, etc. Would it surprise you to know that man, with all of his creative ability, has never created a word which exactly and perfectly portrayed any of his thoughts? This is true, thus man continues to search out a better method of communication, newer and more descriptive words.

There is a word which expresses perfectly the true Self, the Soul of everything that lives. That word, when spoken with understanding, produces a sound which is creative. It will create the form, through control of the vibration of substance, into which a thought is made manifest, thus giving it the proper clothing for its appearance in the Light of Day.

That word is very simple, being composed of just two letters: OM. As an exercise, do the following for a month:

Think consciously:

"I am a Conscious Soul Incarnate."

Then sound the OM, singing it in the key which seems most natural.

The Path of Initiation, Vol. I

Lesson 10

Truth

The Demand to Know,
Aspiring to God for Humanity,
High Noon

In the past nine lessons, I have given you much of great value, much that can be of value to you both as individuals and collectively. In this lesson, I shall speak to you of application, for it is in the process of daily living that any concept is proved or disproved.

As I project these words, it is with great Love in my heart for you, for I know many of your trials, your thoughts, and your aspirations. You are seekers, all of you, seeking Truth as man has sought Truth throughout all of his many experiences. That seeking has been the basic cause of all your experiences, regardless of their nature. The so-called good and the bad have been the result of man's great desire to know. The vague, indescribable restlessness within, which drives man from one experience to the other, is his demand for Truth. And what is the Truth that man seeks? His own Identity. The realization that he is a Son of God, a Conscious Soul Incarnate.

Down through the ages, a man here and there has found that Truth, has established, once and for all, the fact of his own Divinity, and out of a selfless love for his brothers has tried to bring this Truth to all men. Today, the demand to know has risen from the subconscious of the race, and humanity as a whole is conscious of this demand as the great need which must be fulfilled. The spark of aspiration is being fanned into flame, and as world conditions become more critical, that flame can be seen to burn more brightly. As human aspiration surmounts the greed of the separated self, the demand of humanity for Truth will become so powerful as to bring it forth, and man will be free; "Know the Truth, and it shall make you Free."

You can help in this great effort, by uniting with all of those others who are consciously seeking Truth. Realize first, that many individuals and groups are receiving these lessons for the same reason that you are, because they are aspiring to God. Unite with one another on the plane of thought, and aspire to God for all men. Desire that Truth for humanity.

Then realize that not only are there many receiving these lessons, but that there are also many who are finding Truth through other forms of teaching. It is the same teaching, My brothers. It only takes different forms. Then, as a group, unite or become at-one with all of these, and continue your aspiration to God, for all humanity.

The moment of high noon has been set aside throughout the entire world, for the at-one-ment on the planes of thought and feeling of all students of Truth and of all those who serve. You, too, can serve by entering into this activity. Think of the Great Power for Good, which is set into motion by the uniting of minds, for the purpose of aiding man in search for Truth. As you do this, pour forth your Love to all your brothers, as I pour forth my Love to you now. That Love is a tangible reality, and its healing power is great.

In the past nine lessons, we have considered the way in which we create our own world via our thoughts, emotions, sound, and words. This has been done by studying separately each of these activities. Let us complete the act now, by integrating these bits of knowledge into one living Truth, as we apply them to our daily affairs.

Learn to think with clarity, and be choosy as to the thoughts you entertain. Let your emotions be such that you attract Truth into your minds. Learn to formulate that Truth in the proper word symbols, so that your speech can be a tool for service. Let that sound which proceeds from you be harmonious, and another tool for service.

Seek to enter upon the Path of Discipleship by fitting yourself to serve God in the midst of your daily living.

Keep a Spiritual Diary and into this diary put all of the ways in which you have been able to live Truth, to apply it where you are. Do this religiously and as your mind continues to dwell more and more on Truth, you will discover many ways in which you can apply it.

My Brothers, this is the last lesson of this series. Many other series will follow, and those of you who are ready will receive them. As you are ready you will ask, and in asking you will receive.

It is with great Love and understanding, and with a Prayer for your Illumination, that I close this series.

The Path of Initiation, Vol. I

Peace be unto you.

The Path of Initiation

Volume II

Lesson 1

The Soul

Three Aspects,
Conscious Soul Incarnate,
Purpose of Evolution,
Rules of the Path

In any attempt to understand the Soul, it is wise to consider first that which creates the Soul. In occult terminology, they are known as the Will Aspect, and the Intelligence Aspect of Divinity. Orthodox Religion defines them as the Father, and the Holy Ghost, while the scientific mind recognizes them as a Positive Pole and a Negative Pole. All are correct, and yet all fail to convey understanding. The purpose, quality, and expression of Divinity are far beyond man's present mind development. His comprehension cannot grasp so great a Truth, and yet, as he evolves, he will gradually absorb more and more of this Truth, until he becomes himself, Truth.

The Soul is a term given to consciousness. The interplay of energy between the Positive Pole and the Negative Pole creates conscious awareness. Divine Will impregnates the Intelligence of Substance, and so the Soul or Son Aspect comes into being; consciousness is born.

This consciousness contains within itself Divine Will, which is the motivating impulse for evolution, the Will to be, to progress forward; Intelligent Activity, which is the form-building aspect for expression; and Divine Love which is the quality of that expression.

The Soul is, in reality, one Soul manifesting in myriad forms. To be more explicit, we can classify those forms which we recognize as being the mineral kingdom, the vegetable kingdom, the animal kingdom, the human kingdom, and the Spiritual kingdom, or the Kingdom of Conscious Souls Incarnate.

This latter classification is not known by many, so I will take this opportunity to clarify it. When the Soul has evolved over a long period of time, out of the three planes of human endeavor into conscious awareness of reality, it then reincarnates in a physical form. It retains its grasp of reality, its knowledge of one Source, and its ability to manifest its three innate characteristics: Divine Will, Divine Love, and Divine Intelligence. Into this Kingdom pass all the illumined sons of man, and eventually all of humanity will reach this glorious consummation. Then, we will have a race of Conscious Souls Incarnate in form, manifesting perfection in form.

Because of the differentiation of form, and the apparent difference in the evolution of the Soul within different forms, it is difficult for the unenlightened to grasp this concept of oneness. The Soul in all forms, regardless of seeming differentiation, is one Soul with one purpose and one goal. It builds many forms, each one created for the purpose of evolution and expression. Each form, then, conveys a type of Soul expression.

Differentiation in the Soul itself can be explained in the following manner. An individual Soul is an atom in the

Lesson 1

body of the one Soul, which has acquired conscious awareness of itself. It is not in the beginning conscious of the whole, but because of its inherent characteristics, it is swept into incarnation to develop its awareness, and to aid the Over-Soul in its evolution. All of this time, the Whole is aware of the new birth of awareness, and aids it in its long period of growth, until it too, becomes conscious of the Whole.

The purpose of evolution, as far as man's mind has been able to grasp, is At-one-ment, complete with individuality.

I would like to take the opportunity to explain something to the earnest student in regard to his understanding of the teaching. I realize the difficulty presented, particularly to the beginner, in grasping the concept of Truth which is projected. He is confronted with a bewildering array of new and meaningless terms, with concepts new and startling, and with the answers to the reason for his Being, which he had never expected to find. If he is not very careful at this stage, he is liable to become so confused as to what is truth, that he may delay his own growth unnecessarily long.

First, examine very carefully your motives. For what, and why are you seeking? What will you do with this teaching once you have grasped it? Do you have the betterment of mankind in mind, or do you seek for self-glorification?

Remember, the Conscious Soul is part of the Whole. His desire is the evolution of that in which he lives, moves, and has his being. Any activity in which the Soul is engaged is in service to his brothers.

If there are any of you who seek attainment for the glorification of the separated self, it would be better if he dropped out, if he waited until such time as his motives become pure. They will, as he learns through painful experience the emptiness of the illusion about him, the inevitability of change, the dissatisfaction when a long-sought goal is finally reached, and the inability to find fulfillment. All of these painful experiences finally cause man to seek fulfillment in service. His motives become pure, and he is at last ready to begin his long climb up the mount of Initiation.

This path of initiation is strewn with many obstacles, constituting the basic nature of man himself. He must see himself as he is. He must find and overcome those negative qualities within himself which have been acquired in the world of illusion, and are revealed in the Light of the Soul. It takes great courage to meet, see, and overcome that which constitutes the separated self; it takes courage to cut away that part of one's self which separates him from the Soul, and that courage is born of right motive.

The student who does not consider these things, who is not honest with himself, but continues to be motivated by the selfish purpose of the little will, only brings upon himself great suffering. The keynote of the earnest student is harmlessness. See to it that you cultivate this quality if you would escape the pitfalls that encompass so many.

There are certain rules which, if followed, will aid the student who is honest with himself, and who sincerely desires to learn for the sake of others. I will here set them down:

Lesson 1

1. Flexibility of Consciousness—this is more commonly known as an open mind, and it is an attitude of the greatest importance to the aspirant. It is impossible to know all there is to know about any one subject. All truth is relative to a man and his present state of consciousness. Whenever he thinks he has arrived at full and exact knowledge of any one thing, then he has become crystallized in his thinking, and there is nothing that can be done for him. Get the feel of a great field of knowledge which man has not even touched lying back of all things considered factual.

2. Accept only that which evokes a response from the very core of your being. Do not try to accept something which you cannot feel as being truth; neither accept a statement as truth merely because it comes from so-called authority. Do not be blind in your acceptance, but accept that which you see with the inner eye, and feel with the heart as truth.

3. Do not look at that which you cannot accept as something false. Remember, that for the other, it may be the greatest of truth. Simply allow that which you cannot understand and cannot accept to go by. Do not make an issue of it; wait, and later you will see it in the Light of your own Soul and recognize its place in the scheme of things.

4. The Transference of Concepts—this is difficult at first, and extremely important. Remember that a word or a grouping of words is not the concept which it is attempting to convey. It is a door

through which the aspirant may pass into greater understanding. The word attempts to convey reality, but it is not reality itself. An abstract concept cannot be contained in a word or a grouping of words. The mind must be free to pass through the door, into the fullness of the meaning; therefore do not imprison the mind in the description. Attempt to feel the meaning, to sense the depth of that meaning, and to grasp in realization some understanding of it. Then, gradually, the intuition will be awakened and you will become receptive to the transference of concepts. This will eventually supersede the need for words.

Lesson 2

Cycles of Manifestation

Contacting the Master,
Divine Will,
Service

We are now ready to consider the manner in which the Soul manifests itself in form. Much can be learned by a study of the lower kingdoms in nature. We find cycles of manifestation; certain forms coming in and going out according to a cyclic ebb and flow. This great Law of Cycles is the rhythm of all manifestation—that of the Soul incarnating into form, and the activities of the form itself. Each time the Soul comes back into incarnation, the form will be built of a finer grade of matter— be of greater conductivity, and therefore more capable of Soul expression.

The individual, by inquiring into his own cycles of ebb and flow, will discover how to rebuild his instrument into one of greater usefulness. By observation, you can discover when is the natural period for a great deal of outer activity, and when it is the natural period for inactivity—for gathering in of your life energies, rather than an expulsion of them. This, each one must do for himself, for all individuals experience different cyclic patterns.

There are, however, certain universal cycles which can

be utilized by all. The time of the Full Moon, for instance, is a great period of Hierarchical activity. It is the easiest time in which a Master can be contacted by his students, for it is then that his thoughts are turned outward to his group.

The student can take advantage of this period by stilling physical activity and entering into the state of aspiration. To accomplish the contact, the vibratory activity of the student must be in harmony with the vibratory activity of the Master the student desires to contact. This is most easily established by stilling the physical instrument, calming the emotional nature, and aspiring with the alerted mind. If the student could fast or cut down on his intake of food, abstain from social activity, and refuse to become involved in emotional problems, he would be greatly aided in his attempts to contact his Master.

I want you to understand that these instructions do not constitute an order; they are merely suggestions for those who wish to follow them.

The early morning is another period which should be used by every student as the time of meditation. At sunrise, and for some time afterwards, the Soul turns its attention to its instrument. By going into meditation at this time, the student receives a down-flow of Soul energy, which will see him through whatever the day has to offer. Often, he is able to make a contact with his Soul, and receive communication in the form of realization. Later, he will be able to blend his personality consciousness with that of his Soul, during high moments of meditation.

Lesson 2

We find, when we study the vegetable kingdom its type of Soul expression in its harmony of color, its uniformity of size, and its service to man.

In comparing man to vegetable, we find expression of color which manifests as quality, uniformity in brotherhood, and service to the life indwelling form.

It is always wise to make these comparisons, because in doing so, one learns much anent the laws governing manifestation. In studying the ways of nature, one begins to grasp the Law of Cause and Effect, and is therefore, closer to the heart of Being.

The Soul, when it is building its vehicle, forms it according to the needed experience, colors it with the necessary qualities to draw, under the Law of Attraction, the needed lessons and so grows rich in understanding. Each succeeding form or vehicle is capable of greater Soul expression, until finally the Soul builds a form of such a high vibratory frequency that it can carry the full consciousness of the Soul, and so manifest perfection.

What characteristics do we find in the highly developed form? We find, of course, those inherent characteristics of the Soul itself which it is attempting to manifest. They are enumerated and explained as follows:

A. Divine Will: This is not to be confused with the little will of the separated self, which is a distortion of reality.

Divine Will manifests, first, as motive, the Will to Good, and it motivates all of the activities of the Disciple.

You may ask, what is a Disciple? A Disciple is one who has come into conscious awareness of himself as a Soul. He sees all about him in the Light of the Soul—recognizing the Soul in all others, identifying all as one. His activities are based upon the motivating impulse of the Oversoul, which is the evolution of consciousness.

Divine Will manifests secondly as Purpose. The Disciple is aware of the definite purpose in the manifesting conditions about him, and that purpose is identified as service. He recognizes those about him as Souls with whom he has long been associated and to whom he is indebted in some way. He seeks to serve in whatever way he is called upon to do so, and he does this cheerfully with no thought of self.

It might be well to insert here what is really meant by Service. A group of individuals will come up with as many different ideas as to the meaning of this term as there are members of the group, causing an overall distortion in the group consciousness.

1. Service is indicated by the manifesting environment. One does not need to go out into the world, so to speak, in order to find his particular field of service. Your service will find you where you are, so let us dispel all the illusions and glamour which so often blind the aspirant.

2. Service is not an activity of sticking one's nose into another's business, of censoring or reprimanding another for his morals; nor is it an act of giving advice when it has not been asked for.

The Disciple serves his environment by manifesting

that which he is. He brings harmony into the lives of others by becoming a living example of harmony. He shares his wisdom by manifesting that wisdom which he is and within all who contact him. He stimulates Divine Love, because he is Divine Love.

Service is an act of calling forth the perfection of the Soul within all forms. By recognizing perfection, he aids the Soul in bringing it to the attention of the mind. By calling it forth, he aids the Soul in manifesting a perfect vehicle of expression.

An important concept for the aspirant to grasp, is that, within each heart, regardless of manifesting conditions, there is Divinity—that which some call good—and that by concentrating upon that good, its manifestation is aided. The attitude of criticism is not a part of the accepted Disciple, but rather complete tolerance.

A third manifestation of Divine Will is perseverance, and it is a needed asset in the life of any Disciple. He must learn to work without noting immediate results in the world of form and this is a difficult task. The Disciple is so enthusiastic; he has sensed the vision and grasped a portion of the Divine Plan. Very often in the beginning, he feels an urgency, a need for haste. In his attempts to manifest the Plan as he has seen it, he meets with seeming failure—not once, but many times. Often he does not realize that there is no real failure; but that out of seeming failure, success is one step closer.

In his first attempts, he makes blunders, many mistakes and in viewing these, he feels a certain self-disgust, an inadequacy to meet the need of the times.

He forgets that all through this period of trial and error, he is being watched, and trained, and aided wherever possible. He forgets that he will pass out of this period as a skilled worker, one of the dependable Disciples upon whom the Masters pin their hopes for mankind.

There is another factor here to be considered and that is The Law of Cause and Effect. Cause originates on the inner planes, in the world of thought, and effect is the manifestation of activity in form. We find that every situation is an effect of a state of consciousness, and that to change the situation it is necessary to change first the state of consciousness which is its cause. Therefore, the disciple must learn to work from above downward. He must learn to extend his awareness into the mental plane. He has sensed a portion of the Divine Plan; he then works to establish this as a state of consciousness in the mental plane, a condition in the astral, and eventually, activity in the physical.

Very often, there will be a period of apparent chaos manifesting in the physical plane as a result of his efforts, and this is where the beginner becomes discouraged. The wise Disciple realizes that often change will manifest in just this manner, as karma is precipitated and adjusted. He continues his work, maintaining his strength in the calm assurance of his Soul, that all is well. He perseveres until his goal is achieved.

Lesson 3

Divine Love-Wisdom

Right Aspiration,
Rebuilding the Instrument,
Soul Mates,
The Art of Healing

In our last lesson, we had just begun to consider the inherent characteristics of the Soul which could be found expressed through the highly developed form. We had touched upon—and I say touched upon, because an entire book could be given to each of these Divine attributes—the First Aspect, Divine Will. We are now ready to touch upon the Second Aspect of Divinity.

B. Divine Love-Wisdom: For the sake of clarity, let us define the words used to convey this concept. Anything which is Divine, we recognize as pertaining to, or being God.

Love, or the lack of it, can be used to ascertain the quality of the relationship between any two or more individuals or groups of individuals, that quality which determines the activity resulting from two or more being related.

Wisdom, which is an aspect of Divine Love, is very difficult to define, for words are themselves so inadequate. Where the quality of relationship is Divine Love, there is perfect understanding; and where there is perfect understanding, there is perfect application of knowledge. Wisdom, then, is the ability to put concrete knowledge into intelligent activity, the knowing how to apply that which you know.

Divine Love-Wisdom we understand as describing a Divine Relationship in which there is Divine Understanding resulting in Divine Activity.

Particularly in this evolutionary scheme, is Divine Love-Wisdom important, for it is the lesson to be learned, the quality to be perfected by each and every one in this Solar system; in the instrument perfected for service, we find it predominating in the astral vehicle. This energy body, which constitutes the emotional nature of man, is a great transmitter of force which can be, and often is, of a destructive nature. When the Love Aspect is highly developed, however, we find this body a great healer and transmutation agent, and the power factor in the work of manifestation. In this stage, it constitutes the desire body of the Soul, and through the power of right desire, it attracts all that is needed for the Divine work.

We find this manifesting, first, in the consciousness of the would-be Disciple as right aspiration. He has become, over a long period of experience, discontented with that which he has always known. He longs for something else, and not knowing what that something else is, he is driven from place to place, from religion to religion, from philosophy to philosophy in search of Truth.

At last he has recognized that Truth as something

greater than he, or anyone else as a personality, for he has realized that the personality in itself is without purpose. He sees that something else as his own Higher Self, his self in Reality, and to that he aspires.

He endeavors to see the vision of himself as he really is, a Soul, and in so doing, he becomes aware of the vision, at first distorted by the clouds of his own thinking, later clear and beautiful.

After having seen the vision, if only in part, he then sets about to embody it, to become that in manifestation. He undergoes a period of self-discipline in which he fashions his thought life, his emotions, and his physical actions to portray the ideal he has found.

In this manner, the instrument is literally rebuilt. The mental life gradually becomes undistorted by negativity and the unessentials. The emotional life assumes an attitude of serenity, and the physical body is galvanized into right action.

The aspirant, during this period of throwing out of the instrument that which is undesirable and building in that which is desirable, learns to practice harm-less-ness. He lifts the vibratory frequency of his bodies by a strict discipline over his attitude as it regards others. He becomes harmless in thought, word, and deed. Only then, is he ready for initiation.

In reorienting his activities to the life of the Soul, the aspirant finds Divine Love-Wisdom manifesting next as a recognition of others, which is the first step toward the common goal of man, the establishment of brother-hood. He recognizes, first, those of his immediate group as his brothers, and gradually all the connotations of this relationship seep into his consciousness. He experiences the greatest of all gifts, the richness and fullness of the Love of God in Man.

One of the very important steps towards this goal is the attitude of detachment. We have already touched upon this, now we shall consider it in more detail. As an effect of Divine Love, it is actually an attachment to the Soul of all things, which results in a detachment from the form.

As stated before, Disciples who are thrown together in the life of the personality to work out some portion of the Divine Plan and to adjust their karma, often meet with great difficulty. There are differences in personality reactions, differences in opinion, in type and method of work, and in ray make-up. This causes friction where we find the attention focused in the world of form.

That aspirant learns first that his brother is a Soul, and therefore a part of himself. He then learns to attach importance only to the one-ness of the Soul, and to attach no importance to the differences of the personality. This is at first difficult, for after all, the individual has been concerned with the affairs of the personality for many lives. It necessitates a placing of values upon constant realities, rather than changing conditions, an attainment of right perspective.

The aspirant wants to know how. How can such a thing be attained on this plane of existence?

The answer of course is simple; its application not so easy. Once again we go back to the rules for disciples,

Lesson 3

particularly that of non-criticism. The disciple refuses to criticize in thought, word or deed. He goes farther if he is capable, and recognizes neither vice nor virtue in the personality. He shifts his focal point of attention from the personality, which is actually the clothing of the Soul, to the Soul itself, and there he sees and knows reality. He is neither attracted nor repelled by the personality, but is at-one with the Soul; thus right relationship on the plane of the personality is the result, and we find the disciple able to work in harmony with any and every one.

There is a point of danger here which I wish to bring out in order to eliminate one of the greatest obstacles to group relationship.

First, let us realize that all affinity is the result of a transmission of the energy of Divine Love through the various aspects of the personality. The state of consciousness, as it registers the energy, interprets according to its understanding and so reacts. To take two extremes, let us consider the rapist, and the sincere Minister who is down on his knees praying for the salvation of his congregation. The two are reactions to the same force, but from totally different levels of consciousness. The rapist reacts as an animal, for he is little more than that in consciousness. The Minister reacts as a Servant of God from his more enlightened consciousness.

In a group of disciples there are many thought-forms lying both below and on the threshold of awareness. Almost all individuals react to the above mentioned force by desiring above all else a perfect relationship, usually with someone of the opposite sex. This is the cause of the greatest illusion of all, the distorted concept of Soulmate. The individual intuitively knows that somewhere there can be a perfect relationship, a perfect love, and so he evolves the idea of Soulmate. As the power of love sweeps through him, it magnifies his thought-forms, and he is inevitably attracted to another with a similarity of consciousness and a like manifestation of love. Because he is focused in the personality, he misinterprets the relationship, which in truth is brotherhood, as that of Soulmates. The attempt of the personality to direct the expression of Divine Love, in order to realize its desires, always results in disillusion; and therefore we find the two seeking Soulmates elsewhere—and so on and on until the consciousness realizes the perfect love for all.

I tell you this, my brother, because I know the situations which can arise as a result of too great a power and too little an understanding. I realize your great hunger and the many bypaths that hunger can lead to when not rightly directed. It is this distortion of truth which has discredited so many organizations, disrupted so many lives and caused so many unnecessary delays along the Path of Initiation. That you may receive the power of Love along with the light of Love, and so work with understanding, is my prayer for all of you.

The next manifestation of Divine Love-Wisdom which is discovered by the aspirant, is an increasing ability to heal. At this time, I am going to speak of this briefly. Later, we will consider healing in greater detail, for all Disciples, sooner or later, must learn the art of healing.

There are many aspects of healing seldom considered by the individual. The activity is, however, largely the pouring forth of Divine Love-Wisdom from the Source, via the instrument as a channel, to the dis-eased area, the only qualification being the establishment of Divine Law and Order.

The form the healing takes may be any number of activities, the healing of the mind, of the emotional nature, the physical body, or the environment. It may be accomplished via the right use of speech, the right use of thought, or the use of physical activity. The Medical Doctor, the Magnetic Healer, the Christian Science Practitioner, or the Indian Medicine Man — any and all may be channels for the transmission of healing energy.

The prerequisites to an ability to act consciously as a healer are:

1. Selflessness. The ability to work without thought of self.

2. Harmlessness. That harm-less-ness which results from right relationship and purity of motive.

3. Detachment. The ability to divorce one's self from the personality, and so not allow foolish concern to hamper the work.

4. An ability to establish, and maintain, contact with the Soul, so as to work at all times under Divine Guidance.

5. The ability to see and understand karma, and so work in cooperation with the Law.

6. A knowledge of types and qualities of energy, and the wisdom to organize, coordinate, and direct such energies to a specific goal.

The first three, of course, pertain to the three-fold personality acting as a channel, while the last three pertain to the enlightened consciousness acting as a cause. The last three you can do nothing about until you have cultivated and developed the first three as a part of your equipment. Then, you will be capable of consciously carrying the energy that heals. After you have become a perfect channel, you will, through observation of its activity, learn how to direct such energy.[1]

There are, of course, many other manifestations of Divine Love-Wisdom which are joyfully discovered and experienced by the Disciple. However, I feel that you have been given enough to absorb for the present. May you all know the blessings of Divine Love, and may you share those blessings with others.

---

[1] See also: *Healing*, by Lucille Cedercrans

Lesson 4

Intelligent Activity

Chaos,
Polarization,
Contact with a Teacher,
The Observer

We come now to the third inherent characteristic of the Soul found manifesting in the perfected instrument.

C. Intelligent Activity: This Third Attribute is somewhat difficult to describe, for it is an abstraction difficult to put into concrete form, and yet it is the form the activity of expression takes. We have defined Divine Will as being the motivating impulse for evolution or expression, Divine Love-Wisdom as being the quality of expression, and Intelligent Activity as the form expression takes.

In order to better understand this concept, let us consider for a moment the universal Law of Economy. This is the law of the negative electron and has to do with the intelligence of substance. In terms understandable to the aspirant, this means that all substance is intelligent, that it is motivated by Divine Will, held together by the cohesive quality of Divine Love, and swept into activity, the form that activity takes being this third characteristic—intelligence in controlled motion.[1]

The atom of substance we recognize as being the intelligence of substance held in form by a directing Will and the attractive quality of Love. The atomic structure is the blueprint, the framework of the dense form itself. It is the thought-form which has been precipitated into the physical plane, causing the existence of the dense form for just as long as its existence is maintained by the attention of the Soul.

To avoid later confusion, let us establish these facts:

1. That all substance is actually energy, intelligent by nature, and in constant motion.

2. That all form is constructed around a framework, this framework being the atomic structure.

3. That the individual consciousness works through three types of atomic structure, namely:

   a. the physical atom,

   b. the astral atom,

   c. the mental atom,

   having, therefore, three energy bodies of contact with the world in which he lives.

In the life of the aspirant, Intelligent Activity manifests first as apparent chaos. This is the result of an activa-

---

[1] See also: The Disciple and Economy, by Lucille Cedercrans

tion of old forms, plus a mental awakening. The individual has been undergoing a series of experiences which, in one sense, are not seen; they are felt—in pleasure and pain, in happiness and sorrow, and loss and gain, etc. Very often these experiences appear to be unrelated, and without meaning. Then, one day the individual suddenly awakens to the facts of life, so to speak. He realizes that everything he has undergone has been for a definite purpose. He sees a pattern and realizes the Soul as its motivating cause.

He awakens mentally, taking a mental (note the difference between mental and emotional) interest in what is going on about him.

At the same time, he is the recipient of a flow of Divine energies pouring down from the Soul through the various aspects of the personality. This energy activates the desirable, as well as the undesirable, causing a growth of all that lies within the total state of consciousness.

As it passes through the mental aspect, thoughts of self, as well as thoughts of service, expand and grow into manifestation. The tendency to analyze, so evident in the concrete mind, comes out as criticism, superiority, superficial judgment, etc. The mental body is activated, and the individual becomes aware of his own thought life.

As it passes through the emotional nature, all the desires and ambitions still remaining are fanned into a flame, and rise in conflict with the newly awakened aspiration. Very often the student is amazed to find emotions he had never before realized, almost overwhelming him. The so-called good and bad arise in all their power to confront him.

As it passes through the physical aspect and into the
environment, the effects are usually many and varied,
for here in concrete form the mental state of consciousness and the emotional conditions are precipitated.
There may be an appearance of numerous small ill-
nesses, or even a serious illness, while there may be and
often are, healings which appear miraculous to the
onlooker.

In the beginning, the manifestations seem to be in a
state of upheaval, as though one is opposing the other.
They are in reality signs pointing out the path for the
aspirant.

This is the point of danger for the beginner, the trial
accompanying initiation. The result of this trial depends
upon the ability of the aspirant to maintain the attitude
of the observer, and to become a center of stability; and
this, of course, is dependent upon his polarization.

Polarization is the focal point of attention, that aspect
of the personality in which the individual lives, and
from which he directs activity.

The entire work in this stage is to shift the polarization
from the emotional nature to the mental aspect, and to
bring the personality, focused in the mental instrument,
under the guidance of the Spiritual Soul.

An individual who is focused in the emotional nature is
controlled by his emotions and influenced by the emotions of others. He is buffeted about by the energies of
this aspect, which, you will remember, constitute the

power aspect of manifestation. He is controlled by power on the rampage, so to speak, and cannot from here see with that clear, inner vision, because he is blinded by his own desires and various feelings. He is lost in the midst of illusion, actually a part of that illusion, because he is, after all, only an actor in a great play, unaware of himself as an actor. He is suffering the triumphs, and the tragedies of the role he plays, unaware of his true identity.

Many students reading this lesson will wonder how to do this work of lifting the polarization without direct contact with a teacher. I shall answer that question in several ways. Firstly, let us understand that anyone aspiring to the Soul is in direct contact with a teacher, namely his own Soul, and by continued aspiration, he will soon come to recognize the contact.

Secondly, the aspirant is enabled, through his right aspiration, to contact higher levels of awareness, and from these levels draw down those concepts of Truth which provide a sure foundation for his later understanding.

Thirdly, the aspirant learns to recognize experience as a great teacher, and through his efforts to live the Truth which he has grasped, he develops in the school of experience a consciousness rich in understanding. He does this deliberately, in full awareness of the activity, and his everyday life becomes a thing of beauty, regardless of appearances.

It is not easy, my brother, as nothing is really easy until it has been passed over and becomes, in essence, an integral part of the individual. The aspirant, however, who has reached the point of observation which enables him to see those of his activities that are reactions to the form side of life, has within him the ability to lift his polarization into the mental aspect of his nature. Those are the individuals I am most desirous of reaching. For them, I am writing the following instruction. Others who do not understand or perhaps cannot accept that which they are reading, will nonetheless profit, in that they are undergoing preparation for this phase of growth in the very act of reading.

Those for whom this is a definite Light on the horizon, study the following carefully, and in application, expand that Light:

A. Decentralize Yourself:

You have for a long period of time been the center of your own little stage. This has been good, and has been instrumental in the past growth. However, it is now an impediment to your further progress.

You have, if your past development has been correctly impulsed, acted solely in response to selfish motives. All of your so-called altruistic tendencies, your loves, sympathies, etc. have revolved around you. In a sense, the entire universe has, in your mind, been revolving around you, constructed with no other purpose than to aid or hinder you.

To clarify this concept, ask yourself the following questions:

    1. Has the love of my life really been directed outside of myself to others, or has the relationship

been based upon the desire of my personality? Have I loved giving freedom to the loved one, or has my love taken the form of chains binding others to me for my satisfaction?

Remember, that true love asks no reward, not even love returned.

2. The enemies in my life, why have I had them? Why have I ever felt resentment for others? Has it not been because I, the little I, felt alone and badly treated? Did I ever put myself in the shoes of the other, and consider myself from this point of view?

The Christ said, "Love your enemies."

3. The tragedy of my life, the loved ones who have passed, why do I mourn? Is it really for them, or is it for myself?

Yes, you have long been the center of your own specially constructed stage. Almost every activity has been but the response of the personality to its own form nature. It has assumed such importance in your eye as to completely separate you in awareness from your brother. What is a selfish motive but that which sets you apart from others?

It takes courage, my brothers, to answer those questions, and to face the picture of yourself that you portray.

B. Establish the Attitude of the Observer:

Lift yourself out of the emotional nature. Realize that it is a distinct aspect of your personality, and that it will continue its usual activities without your help. Just sit back and watch it react to conditions. Observe its habits, its sudden storms, its likes, its dislikes. Keep completely apart from this sudden strange aspect of yourself, and learn through observation its purpose, and, eventually, how it can be controlled.

As you do this, you will suddenly discover the cause of much that has happened to you. Your life will quickly assume a definite pattern, and above all, you will learn that you are not your emotions.

All of the above is Intelligent Activity. When you can see it as that, then you are one step closer to the consciousness of the manipulator, rather than that of the manipulated. Think on this, for it is important.

Lesson 5

Characteristics of The Soul

Adaptability and Resistance,
The Observer,
Form Building

In this lesson, we are still considering the third inherent characteristic of the Soul found manifesting in and through the perfected form.

Intelligent Activity manifests secondly as adaptability. The aspirant learns to adapt himself to his environment, and finally to adapt his environment to the best that is within him. He and his environment slowly adjust to the Soul, and so Divine Law and Order reasserts itself, first within his consciousness, then within his environment. Right relationship is the result. A clue can be given the earnest student in the following words:

> *"Alone I stand upon the scale, and reaching out, I bring into all relationships that peculiar motion which results in balance."*

Once again, it would be wise to consider the world in which you live. It is in a constant state of flux. That which today appears constant and unchanging, is tomorrow a thing of the past, giving way to the new. All form is temporary, ever passing, ever assuming new patterns, and these changing in the very act of forming.

Consciousness grows through its ability to adapt to the changing conditions about it. Contrary to average thought, it is not resistance which produces growth, but rather adaptation—that capacity which allows consciousness to lend itself to a manifesting condition and to come through whole and unharmed. This can be seen in war in the case of bodily harm, such as the removal of a limb, etc., and any one of the manifesting conditions in the world of form. Even though the consciousness may be unaware of this ability to adapt, it constantly does so, and when that adaptation can be conscious, we see rapid growth.

The aspirant, once he grasps this fact, realizes that while he as a personality, may have been resisting conditions within his environment, his consciousness has been lending itself to them. Following this example, the aspirant then stops fighting and begins to cooperate with his consciousness. He enters into the condition, but he does so in a detached manner, first as an observer, later as an actor. The latter he does only after he is fully aware of his Soul purpose for that particular incarnation.

He recognizes his first reactions of resistance as activity directed by the personality and, therefore, relatively unintelligent. He withdraws the personality from the field of action and enters it as the observer. He quietly enters into his environment, seeing in it only good, and that environment slowly, but surely, responds to the flow of positive energy exerted upon it.

Many volumes could be written anent this aspect of Intelligent Activity, but until the aspirant can grasp this one concept, and see the difference between resistance and adaptation, they would be of no value to him. For this reason, I strongly urge each sincere student to meditate and reflect upon the meaning of the concept, as a preparation for later lessons. This meditation and reflection, if carried out over a period of one year, will provide a secure foundation from which to proceed.

It would be to your advantage to keep a double ledger, one side a record of that activity which can be noted as resistance, the other side a record of that activity which can be noted as adaptation. Thus will your thinking be clarified.

The third manifestation of Intelligent Activity which we shall consider at this time can be seen in the growing ability of the aspirant to engage in the art of form-building.

The aspirant learns to see all form as substance in con-trolled motion, created to convey a purpose and result in a desired goal. The individual's own form is then regarded as an instrument. Its purpose is eventually revealed, and its goal is seen. The qualities which that form has been specially constructed to portray are real-ized, and the aspirant then sets out to build those forms which will further the expression of the Soul. Several points should here be remembered:

1. The form is Intelligent Activity made manifest.

2. All activity in manifestation takes form on one or many planes.

As an example, speech is one form the activity of thought takes, as thought is made manifest on the physical plane.

Its purpose is communication or relationship.

Its goal is unity or at-one-ment.

The aspirant observes all of his activities, noting the particular form each one tends to take. Recognizing as an example, the form his thought takes in speech, he sees his own thought portrayed in speech, notes the quality of the thought which is, after all, a form of higher expression, and the clarity and the desirability of the words used to portray that thought.

This brings him to the sudden realization that his intelligent activity has been carried out in a rather hit-or-miss sort of way. He then sets out to put a semblance of order into it.

1. He guards his speech and in doing so, becomes more cognizant of his thought-life. He becomes aware of the type, strength, and quality of mental energy with which he is constantly working, as well as his right or wrong use of it. He learns the purpose of his mental aspect, recognizing it as an instrument of the Soul, and at the same time, as the body of cause for lower manifestations. He sees it as an intermediary between a higher consciousness and a lower consciousness, and not as the consciousness itself. It becomes to him, then, what it is in reality: a type of substance which receives electric impulse, transposes that impulse into picture-form in mental matter, and transmits the picture-form into physical manifestation via the use of sound. The

word is made flesh.

2. He disciplines his physical activity to conform to his mental picture of Soul purpose. He recognizes that activity which is a response to the form side of life, and that which is a response to the Soul. He sees all past activity as being either a vehicle of expression for the higher or the lower consciousness, and he learns that activity which blends or merges the two states of consciousness into one. Right action is analogous to the marriage ceremony, since it weds the two into one, and thus man becomes in awareness a Living Soul.

In later lessons, you will receive specific instructions as to methods of procedure in the art of form building. In the meantime, acquaint yourselves with the over-all concept, with the terminology, and apply your expanding knowledge in your present activities.

See within each activity presented, an opportunity to express a Soul quality, and seize that opportunity through right action. In meditation, hold yourselves receptive to higher impulse, and pour into your activities the energy of the impulse received. In this manner, you will expand and grow in cooperation with the Law.

Peace Be Unto You

The Path of Initiation, Vol. II

Lesson 6

Three Types of Energy

Desire and Aspiration,
Disillusion,
Alignment

We have enumerated and defined the three inherent characteristics of the Soul found manifesting in and through the perfected form as Divine Will, Divine Love-Wisdom, and Intelligent Activity. We have considered at some length these attributes as the main factors of influence in the aspirant's treading of the Path. We realize now that the aspirant is impulsed by the Divine Will of the Soul, infused and illuminated by the Divine Love-Wisdom of the Soul, and swept into activity by the ‚Divine Intelligence of the Soul

We shall now consider these three attributes as being three types of vibratory energy which reach and influence the aspirant according to his aspiration, meditation, and application. We shall consider at some length this three-fold method of contacting, accepting, and embodying the divine energies of the Soul. This will give the student a further understanding of the Law, and make it possible for his eventual contact in awareness with his Soul.

A. Aspiration: What do we mean by this term? In order to clarify its meaning, we shall begin with a consideration

of its correspondence on a lower level, namely—
Desire.

Desire, which is found to predominate in the emotional
nature of the personality, is based upon the selfish will
of the brain.

I wish to insert here what is meant by our use of the
word "selfish" in order to avoid a misinterpretation of
those reading these lessons. We are not concerned with
the so-called good and bad which characterizes this
term as used by humanity as a whole. Anything which
concerns the separated self, we consider as being selfish. Certainly, much of the so-called good and bad are
results of this attitude. It is the attitude of exclusion,
and can be, at times, very subtle and difficult for the
aspirant to see within himself.

The desire to attainment is selfish and characterizes
almost all probationers on the path. It separates the
individual in awareness from his brother. A barrier of
thought and emotion is revolving around him in such a
manner as to cut him off from others. Thus, he is ren-
dered insensitive to anything which does not have a
direct impact upon him as a separated, all-important
personality.

The aspirant recognizes and eliminates this personality
trait by realizing, first, that he is a part of a whole, and
that he is dependent upon each part of and upon the
whole. He then realizes that he is important (and important is an incorrect term) only in-so-far as his relationship to each part, and to the whole, is recognized
and rightly balanced.

Lesson 6

We shall now go back to our consideration of desire: the selfish will which centers itself in the little "I", seated in the brain, to the emotional polarization located in the region of the solar plexus, via the nervous system. This calls forth from the emotional nature a vibratory energy activity which is commonly called desire.

The emotional body of most persons, as seen by a clairvoyant, is in an almost constant state of turmoil. There are vortices of energy, very similar to the whirlpools in a stream or river, into which the energies of the individual are pulled. These vortices represent the various desires which tend to pull the individual first this way, and then that.

They are spasmodically stimulated by the little will impulse, but without a definite rhythm, being therefore somewhat unpredictable and erratic. In this case, we see the individual who is completely ruled by his emotions, who is without purpose, and a victim of so-called circumstance at all times.

There is a difference when there is desire coupled with purpose. The individual then tends to become one-pointed in his desire, and there is less turmoil in the emotional body. The vortices will be confined to one or two large ones and a more definite rhythm will be established. This rhythm attracts and repels, and so we see periods of intense desire, with later gratification by the fulfillment of that desire.

The gratification of desire always leads, sooner or later, to disillusion, and so the individual still remains dissatisfied. This naturally leads to a substitution of goal, and a new period of intense desire, until such time as the individual awakens to the fact that desire is a betrayer. He then turns from it, and gradually enters into a state of aspiration.

In summing up desire, we say it is an activity of the emotional nature impulsed by the selfish will of the personality. It is always separative, being confined to the satisfaction of the individual concerned, and therefore largely responsible for the lack of brotherhood in the world today.

Aspiration is the result of an electrical impulse projected from the Soul (focused in the region of the heart) via the energy underlying all substance. Thus, is the vibratory activity of the emotional nature quickened, and this aspect literally lifted up out of the lower level where desire characterizes it to the higher levels of aspiration.

We then see a body of energy which is relatively quiescent, characterized by a radiatory activity which is both expansive, and contractive.

We have, then, an impulse from the Soul which stimulates the aspiration into being. The aspirant begins by a sort of longing, a yearning toward the Light. Just as a flower reaches toward the light of the sun, so the aspirant reaches toward the Light of the Soul.

Just as a flower grows and blooms, and radiates beauty, so does the aspirant grow and bloom, and radiate Divinity. This radiation of the aspirant is characterized by his giving, in the form of activity, of the energies he has received from the Soul. This continual reaching toward the Light, and in turn, the giving or sharing of that

Lesson 6

Light, has been termed aspiration.

This, in turn, evokes a further response from the Soul, and the aspirant is the recipient of greater Light. In this manner, through a cyclic ebb and flow of energies— a call from the personality, response from the Soul and vice versa—we see man bloom as a Soul-infused personality.

The slang phrase, "man lifts himself up by his bootstraps", is a very good analogy for this activity in which all aspirants are engaged.

The term itself, "aspirant" , as applied to an individual, denotes a certain development, and is not carelessly used in connection with all students. The aspirant is one who is engaged in the evocation of the Divine Will impulse.

This is most important and should be contemplated by all sincere students. Only in this manner can the First Aspect of Divinity be brought into active manifestation within the individual environment.

When the aspirant is well into this phase of growth, his mental attitude can best be described by the following words:

"Not my will, Oh Soul, but Thine."

Deliberately, and often at great seeming cost to the personality, is the call sounded forth. The little will of the personality, which has ruled for a long period of time, is subordinated to the Will of the Soul, and not without battle.

Those forms which are out of harmony with Soul purpose are destroyed, and remember this destruction includes any discordant form, whether it be a thought-form, emotion, a physical form, or an activity form. Thus, is the attention of the aspirant lifted up, and the eye opened.

I shall speak of alignment at this time, for it is here that it is first consciously put to use.

Alignment is the establishment of a path for the flow of energies between any two points. It is the path of least resistance for any manifesting activity.

The aspirant aligns himself with the Will of the Soul, and this he does in the following manner:

1. He recognizes, first, the fact of the existence of the Soul.

2. He mentally and emotionally accepts the Will of the Soul.

3. He visualizes a line of Light reaching out from his brain, extending through his mind to his Soul. Along this line, the call is sent.

Evocation is a calling forth, and when done correctly, the response is inevitable. A vibration is set up along this line which reaches the Soul and commands its attention. The answer is then sent forth.

It is important for the student to realize that his response does not come in the form of words spoken into the brain. It is, at first, nothing more than a subtle change of, and in, his activities, and the presentation of opportunity via activity or lack of activity.

Most students are so busily engaged in looking for, and thinking about unusual phenomena that they fail to register and recognize the more subtle influence of the Soul. Remember, we spoke of Divine Will impulse; this is an actuality. It is an electrical impulse, the impact of which changes the vibratory frequency of the aspirant's instrument, and in this manner, produces change in his thoughts, emotions, words, deeds, and environment.

4. He maintains this line of contact at all times, subordinating his activities and his personal will to the Divine Will of the Soul.

In considering this lesson, and its application, remember that we are concerned with *aspiration* and not meditation. The alignment given should not, at this time, be any more than a mental activity which is simultaneous with the routine of daily living. Let the eyes remain open, the brain subjectively attentive, and the physical instrument outwardly busy as usual. Do not use this alignment given as a meditation form.

In summing up aspiration, we say it is an activity of the higher emotional nature and the mind, which is impulsed by the Soul. It is always concerned with the Divine Plan, being therefore inclusive, and eventually producing within the mind and the heart of the aspirant, the recognition, acceptance and practice of Brotherhood.

The Path of Initiation, Vol. II

Lesson 7

Energies of The Soul

Meditation, Relaxation,
Focus, Soul Contact,
Cycles and Correspondences

In order to quickly establish continuity of the lesson material projected, I shall refer back to the first two paragraphs of Lesson 6.

We have enumerated and defined the three inherent characteristics of the Soul found manifesting in and through the perfected form as Divine Will, Divine Love-Wisdom, and Intelligent Activity. We have considered at some length these attributes as the main factors of influence in the aspirant's treading of the Path. We realize, now, that the aspirant is impulsed by the Divine Will of the Soul, infused and illumined by the Divine Love-Wisdom of the Soul, and swept into activity by the Divine Intelligence of the Soul.

We shall now consider these attributes as being three types of vibratory energies which reach and influence the aspirant according to his aspiration, meditation, and application. We shall consider at some length, this three-fold method of contacting, accepting, and embodying the Divine energies of the Soul. This will give the student a further understanding of the Law, and make it possible for his eventual contact in awareness with his Soul.

B. Meditation: Meditation, when rightly carried out, brings the aspirant into contact with the illuminating aspect of the Soul. It makes possible the recognition, and the eventual embodiment of the quality of the Soul.

We have, first, the state of aspiration which puts the student in tune, so to speak, with the Soul, after which meditation is added to the student's daily routine.

Many students have come to their teachers with various questions as to what meditation is, and how it can be carried out. Few, if any of them, have other than a distorted concept of the activity, and a great many of them have further confused the subject by attempting to carry out what they think, or what someone has told them, meditation is.

Meditation is communion with the Soul or higher states of consciousness. It is a freeing rather than a straining of the personality consciousness. This is a point to be remembered. Any meditation which is either hurried or strained will not result in Soul contact. It will merely serve to render the body and the mind uncomfortable.

The first step in any well-ordered meditation is alignment. We have already defined alignment in a former lesson, as the establishment of a path for the flow of any two given points. In this case, the alignment must be between the lowest aspect of the personality and the Soul, through the other aspects of the personality. This establishes a path for the flow of Soul energies in whatever form is in Divine Law and Order.

Lesson 7

The personality is composed of three major aspects: the physical or dense body, the astral or emotional nature, and the mind or mental nature.

The objective of the first stage of alignment is to render the physical body, and the emotional nature, quiescent and under complete mental control. This is brought about in a two-fold manner as follows:

1. Relaxation: The physical body and the emotional nature must be completely relaxed. Wherever there is tension, there the mind is held a prisoner. If the emotional nature is tense, there is a corresponding physical tension. These tensions hold the attention of the mind fastened to the body and the problem, without freedom to seek, recognize, or create a solution. Any attempt to strain or lift the mind from its prison will only serve to strengthen its hold; therefore the process must be one of relaxing, which results in a freeing of the mind. This is accomplished in the following manner:

    a. Become physically relaxed and comfortable. It is best to do this in a sitting position. Make the body as comfortable as is possible. Beginning with the feet, relax each muscle, tendon, and finally cell of the entire body. Speak to the separate parts, telling them to relax and know that the nervous system carries this message to them, and that they will obey.

    b. Become emotionally calm and serene. Speak to the emotions, telling them to relax and to become at peace. Let each worry, etc., slip away until there is a noticeable calming of the emotions.

2. Focus: When the physical body and the emotions are quiescent, the personality consciousness is naturally focused in the mind nature. The mind, which is no longer held a prisoner to the lower aspects, naturally focuses its attention in the world of mind. It does not leave the body, but it does become attentive to the Soul. It is poised and alert. This can be best facilitated in the following manner:

   a. Establish a deep, easy, rhythmic breath, that which seems natural and comfortable.

   b. Taking seven deep breaths, the student lets his mind (attention) rise from the body and emotions and focuses it in the center of the forehead (between the brows).

Do not create a point of tension here; simply settle easily in the forehead. You are now focused in the mind. You have aligned the physical body and the emotional nature with the mind.

The next step is to align the mind with the Soul. In the past, beginners have made the mistake of trying too hard. Let us eliminate that mistake now. Do not try to place the locality of the Soul. It is everywhere equally present, and to place it before recognition and understanding only limits your thinking. Instead, align yourself with the Soul by turning your attention to the concept of the Soul. Simple? Yes, Truth is ever simple.

Lesson 7

You are now aligned with the Soul. You are ready to enter into communication with the Soul. This is done in the following manner.

Your mind is fixed upon the concept of a Soul. This concept is bridged by a seed-thought. The mind is given a thought which quickens its vibratory frequency in such a manner as to span the distance in awareness between it and the Soul. Thus, the mind is in contact with the Soul.

A very good seed-thought for all beginners is:

"I Am my Soul; My Soul I Am."

This identifies and serves to merge the two states of consciousness, the Soul and the personality, in time and space.

The seed-thought is then dropped. The words are no longer spoken. This is the most difficult stage of the entire meditation for beginners and Disciples alike. The tendency of the mind to repetition swings the student into the habit of affirmation, and this is the exact opposite of the condition required for Soul contact. Just so long as the mind is speaking, it is closed to communion with the Soul. It must become quiet, attentive, alert.

The seed-thought is dropped as words. The energy of the thought remains as a line of communication, and needs no repetition.

The mind is stilled. When the moment of absolute silence is reached, the Soul makes itself known.

I should like to insert a few words of warning. Cast out from your mind all the preconceived ideas you have formulated as to what Soul contact is. You have probably heard stories of various phenomena experienced during meditation. Some of the common ones are a burst of bright light, communication in the form of words, visual pictures, etc. This is all well and good, and may be true of the individuals concerned, but it is not a criterion.

Each individual experiences his contact in an individual manner. Some never see light, never see pictures, never hear or sense words. All of these ways or forms are dictated by the personality, not the Soul. The purest form of Soul communication is that of instantaneous knowing. Anything else is a means, not the goal.

Accept that which comes as the method best suited to your development, and do not covet another's way. This is most important.

If you will remember, we spoke of the Law of Cycles in an earlier lesson, touching very briefly upon it as one of the controlling factors in all manifestation. We shall consider it once again in more detail as regards meditation—for meditation, to be fruitful, must be carried out in a cyclic pattern. There are cycles within cycles, and in order to bring clarity to the concept, we shall go from the general to the specific.

All forms appear in time and space in cycles, those cycles being peculiar to the entity manifesting the form. A solar system appears in dense form over a long period of time, and at the end of its cycle of activity disappears from the Light of Day, to rest for an equal length of time. Thus, we have a Solar Day and Night. During the Solar Day, the activities of the entire system manifest in cyclic periods peculiar to the form the activity takes. Thus, the Day progresses, and is completed.

Within the Solar entity are lesser lives which manifest in form according to this same Law. A Planetary Life comes into form, manifests certain activities in relation to those of other lives, and withdraws from form until its next cyclic period of activity.

This is true of all consciousness, the cycle of the higher always affecting the lower, but allowing the lower a certain amount of freedom to manifest its individual cycles contained within the larger. During the Solar Day, planetary entities come in and out in a cyclic manner peculiar to the entity concerned, but being affected always by the cycles of the Solar entity itself, and the Solar entity being affected by the cyclic manifestation of the Cosmos, etc.

Within the Planetary Life are contained many lesser lives, among which are the five kingdoms in nature. These kingdoms are, each one, an entity containing many lesser lives. We see the vegetable kingdom, as an example, manifesting in form over a long period of time. Within this larger cycle of manifestation are the lesser cycles which govern the appearance of various members of the One Life. There are the seasons, during which certain forms of vegetable life come in and go out in cycles peculiar to the member.

The human kingdom manifests in the same manner. The human entity appears over a long period of time during which certain states of consciousness come in and go out according to the Law of Cycles. While a state of consciousness is in the process of manifestation, degrees or levels of that consciousness come in and go out; thus we see the rise and fall of civilizations, of races, nations, governments, organization, family lines, etc.

Contained within the level of a state of consciousness are the lesser lives, the individual human entities who appear in form in a cyclic pattern peculiar to the Human Kingdom, the state of consciousness, the degree or level of consciousness, and finally to the individual himself.

Within the cycle of individual incarnation are the lesser cycles governing his activities. These cycles are harder to determine and understand for they are affected by all larger cycles which have produced the opportunity for incarnation, and by those individual cycles governing the activities of his associates. He must come to understand the larger cycles which provide him with opportunity for growth in certain directions, as well as to establish his rhythm in harmony with the rhythm of others, thus manifesting right relationship.

The aspirant is oft overwhelmed with the enormity of the task, but it is not so difficult as it appears. It does call for a higher concept to be held in the student's mind, as well as a broader point of view, and therefore a change in his thinking processes. The beginner would do well to apply the Law of Correspondence to all that he sees about him. Through observation and application of this Law, much will be grasped and understood which cannot be explained to him in words.

We shall now proceed to the Law of Cycles and its effect

upon meditation. Remember, as we proceed, that the individual cycles are contained within the larger, and that the individual must find and establish his own rhythm in right relation to others.

At present, we shall consider meditation as a three-fold process, considering only those cycles which affect this three-fold manifestation. The concept and the resulting activity will have to be enlarged as the student progresses along the path to initiation. It would be well for the student to remember this in regard to all of the teaching, so as not to become crystallized in his thinking to the point of non-receptivity.

The three-fold process of meditation can best be described in three words:

1. Reception

2. Absorption

3. Precipitation

The beginner must carry out his meditation in a cyclic pattern which provides a period for each of the Three Aspects. Later—much later—his meditation will include the three-fold process as a simultaneous activity in one period.

The period of reception is that period of time during which realizations are received in the consciousness of the aspirant. This may cover any period of time from hours to days, weeks, or in rare instances even months. During this period, the personality is the recipient of the illumining quality of the Soul. His entire nature responds to this period. He is alert, expectant, and joyful.

For the average humanity, probationers, and beginners on the Path of Discipleship, this period usually begins two weeks before the Full Moon, and progresses so that the time of greatest realization is in the vicinity of the Full Moon. The smaller cycle of reception contained within the larger, for the same group, covers the period from sunrise until high noon. This is not a criterion, however, for today we find many levels of consciousness manifesting together in time and space, each one having its own peculiar rhythm.

The period of absorption is that time during which the aspirant does not receive new realizations, but absorbs into himself the energies of the realizations received during the period of reception. This period of time is a variable, and even an example may be confusing if the student does not remember that this cycle of absorption will be peculiar to himself, and perhaps differ from that of anyone he knows. It may cover a very long period of time, or a very short one, depending upon the condition of his bodies, his peculiar ray make-up, his karmic obligations, etc.

During the age from which we are now passing, this period covered the two weeks following the Full Moon, and contained within it the activity of precipitation. The lesser cycle covered the period from high noon until sunset. This is still true of some, but all New Age Souls who fall into this classification of teaching, manifest a shorter period of absorption, and a separate period of precipitation.

The attitude during this period should be one of contemplation and reflection. The aspirant turns over in his mind the realization he has received, thus absorbing the accompanying energies. He embodies Light.

The period of precipitation, which is a New Age manifestation in itself, is the period of time during which the aspirant proves the Truth of his realization. He precipitates that which has been received and absorbed into his environment. He builds a living structure of Truth through his efforts of application in physical plane experience. There the structure stands for all to see.

This cycle is such a variable that I shall not even give an example. Each one must find his own rhythm.

A seed-thought should cover the full time containing the three periods. An individual who changes his seed-thoughts before its results have been absorbed and precipitated throws his meditation out of balance, and may not receive further realization for a long time to come.

Keep a diary or record of your meditation results. In this manner, you will be able to observe your own natural cycles and utilize them with Wisdom.

A later, more advanced lesson on meditation will be forth-coming when you are ready to receive it.

Let There Be Light.

The Path of Initiation, Vol. II

Lesson 8

Application

Living the Truth,
Thought, Speech,
and Action

Once again, I shall refer you back to the first two paragraphs of Lesson 6.

We have enumerated and defined the three inherent characteristics of the Soul found manifesting in and through the perfected form as Divine Will, Divine Love-Wisdom, and Intelligent Activity. We considered at some length these attributes as the main factors of influence in the aspirant's treading of the Path. We realize, now, that the aspirant is impulsed by the Divine Intelligence of the Soul.

We shall now consider these three attributes as being three types of vibratory energy which reach and influence the aspirant according to his aspiration, meditation, and application. We shall consider at some length, this three-fold method of contacting, accepting, and embodying the Divine energies of the Soul. This will give the student a further understanding of the Law, and make possible his eventual contact in awareness with his Soul.

C. Application: After a careful study of Lessons 6 and

7, we know that the Will Aspect of the Soul is contacted by the student's persistent aspiration, and that the Love-Wisdom Aspect is contacted by the aspirant's ability to meditate. The Third Aspect, that of Intelligent Activity, we now learn is contacted by the applied effort of the aspirant to *live* Truth.

This application put forth by the aspirant not only brings his life and affairs into Intelligent Activity, but it also makes it possible for him to manifest in activity the other two aspects of the Soul which he has contacted.

In order to arrive at an understanding of how this is done, and what is actually meant by us in our use of the word "application", we shall consider the Disciple's ability to establish and control his vibratory activity.

We have, in earlier lessons, defined a Disciple as one who has entered into conscious awareness of himself as a Soul, and who works in the world as such.

The "work" of the Disciple can best be described as his establishment of a certain type and quality of vibratory impact upon his environment, and his control at all times of that impact.

The new student immediately wants to know what is meant by vibratory impact. You, your thoughts, words, emotions, and deeds carry a certain vibratory frequency, and as this frequency comes in contact with another individual, or group of individuals, the effect is called vibratory impact. The impact of your vibration upon others can be either harmonious, or discordant. When the effect is harmonious, the individuals are in right relationship.

decree has been made. That word, or grouping of words, will manifest in time and space. My friends, could you but see the effect produced by your words, you would be shocked. The broken bodies, the sick emotions, the chaotic conditions which result from the words spoken by humanity are painful to look upon by those with vision. A word once spoken cannot be recalled. A chain of effects has been set into motion, and will result in physical plane manifestation.

The aspirant speaks, and because he has become a recipient of a certain amount of Soul energy, his words manifest with greater strength and speed than do those of his less-evolved brothers. His words have a definite influence upon those within his environment. His words form and shape the conditions in which their younger brothers must live. Many of the obstacles the younger brother must meet and overcome were laid at his feet by the little-knowing aspirant.

My brother, guard your speech. Study its effects upon others, and learn harmlessness. You cannot advance upon the Path until this lesson is learned.

3. Emotions: This subject presents quite a problem, for the average beginner has little or no understanding of the emotions. Emotion is the name given to his feelings, and what is a feeling? Lack of proper terminology further complicates the task, hence the lack of clear teaching anent this subject down through the past ages.

Let us proceed by first defining emotion. Emotion is the effect produced by the impact of astral energy upon the sensory system of the physical body and its surrounding environment.

Astral energy is that cohesive energy which, when set into motion, brings together the energy of the mind and the energy of the physical substance, thereby producing form. Astral energy is set into motion by thought, sound, and the activities of the physical instrument. A thought which is held in the mind in sufficient strength produces a like vibration in the astral body. The vibration within the astral body gives the thought a form in astral substance. The vibratory impact of that form upon the sensory system produces what we call an emotion, according to its strength, type, and quality.

Herein lies a key for the earnest student: the registration of an emotion, for the Disciple, is an indication of a thought to which he has given form within his own astral body. It revolves around him, feeding upon his own life energy, coloring his personality experiences, and often controlling his consciousness to the extent of dictating his every act.

For average humanity, the astral or emotional nature is composed of many such forms which completely blind him to the world of reality. Any vibratory impact upon his sensory apparatus (of which his brain is a part) is colored by these forms, distorting the true vibration according to the astral form or forms in control.

The astral plane contains the aggregate of human emotion, and has been called the world of illusion, for here in form are all of man's thoughts concretized and made manifest. All of these thoughts live and have their separate existences on the astral plane. Little wonder that it has been called the plane of illusion. Wise must be the consciousness who enters and works therein.

These astral forms manifest in time and space in a cyclic pattern, and according to the revitalization they receive from the human family. Herein lies a key to one of the world problems. As an individual accepts and entertains a form originated within the astral consciousness of the race, he gives it the power of his own emotion and strengthens its attraction to the physical plane.

The astral forms (emotions for the beginner) we now know have a life of their own, manifest in time and space, and have an effect upon all other lives.

The aspirant at this stage of development must first clean up his emotional nature. He learns which of his emotions produce a harmful effect upon others, and these he eliminates from his vibratory activity by a strict discipline over his emotional nature.

By taking a positive action through the application of kindliness, friendliness, love, and tolerance, his emotional aspect becomes a tower of strength, a healer, and eventually an agent of transmutation for others.

See to this part of yourself, Oh Disciple, for it must become harmless as the dove before the door is opened.

4. Physical Actions: Each act performed by the physical instrument carries a vibratory frequency, the impact of which exerts an influence upon the environment. Physical motion is the result of an expenditure of energy, and that energy once set into motion becomes the cause for a se-

ries of effects. We find that all physical action is an effect of higher cause—astral, mental, or spiritual. The effect always becomes the cause for other effects. All manifestation is the result of energy moving through the various vibratory planes.

Physical action becomes the cause of the effect known as re-action. A mental, emotional, or physical re-action will be the result of any physical activity, unless those who encounter the vibratory impact are capable of transmutation.

When the aspirant ceases the outer activity for a sufficient length of time to contemplate the inner meaning of and for his instrument and its various parts, much revelation comes to him.

The first and most obvious fact is that his physical body is an instrument of contact with the vibratory plane in which his consciousness is focused. Its constitution includes a sensory apparatus for the registration of incoming vibrations, as well as outlets for the release of outgoing vibration. It is a receiving and sending instrument composed of those parts which are tuned to receive and send vibrations which fall within a certain frequency range. Thus, he sees, hears, touches, tastes, and smells, and, in turn is seen, heard, touched, tasted and smelled.

It is interesting to note here that as the vibratory frequency of the instrument is quickened, other senses are experienced, such as telepathy, and all other so-called extra-sensory perceptions.

Lesson 8

The next obvious fact is that he, as a state of consciousness functioning through a physical instrument, is intimately related to all others. This relationship is most easily demonstrated in his ability to communicate. That he has something to communicate to others, and that he can be understood by them is his first conscious realization of relationship.

The average man's lack of belief or faith in a life after death, or in the existence of a Soul, is based upon his inability to communicate with either those who have passed over or with the Soul. As soon as a way is found to perceive and communicate with these, and other states of Being, the Human entity will not only believe, but he will know. An event is coming which will establish once and for all in the race mind the fact of planes of existence other than the physical. The "event" will, of course, concern a type of perception and communication.

The next realization the consciousness experiences is the quality of his relationships. With some, the quality is Love, others, dislike, etc.

If the aspirant will observe that which he communicates to others, he will come to understand that the quality of his relationships is wholly dependent upon himself. He it is who determines the quality of his relationships with another—first in his thoughts, his words, his emotions, and his deeds.

A very good example of this statement is the man who suddenly realizes that the quality of his relationships is deceit. He is lied to, lied about, misrepresented, mistrusted, and mistrusting. Through observation, he discovers that he is communicating this quality to others, and in turn, evoking the same from them. Often he is thinking one thing, and speaking another, or speaking one thing while feeling and acting something else. Thus, his own vibratory activity is out of harmony, and the discord is taking the form of deceit.

The next realization occurs when the aspirant becomes aware of the inner purpose of his instrument and its various parts. As an example, he looks at this hands, and realizes, in part, their reason for being. These God-given instruments were constructed for a Divine Purpose. How well has that purpose been fulfilled?

The hands are first and foremost the channels of Divine energy. Through the hands flow the energies of Divine Love, which, when rightly directed, heals and blesses. The aspirant learns to direct that force outward, through receiving and sharing rather than taking and holding. This is the first lesson the hand teaches. Many others follow.

The eyes are usually the next part of the instrument to be observed. For what Divine Purpose were they constructed? The eyes were constructed to receive and register the beauty of God's Plan on earth. Little more need be said.

Little by little the aspirant observes the various members of his own instrument, learning the inner meaning underlying them, and through self-imposed discipline making of them fit instruments for the Soul. He learns to wield Spiritual energies for the betterment of mankind.

Lesson 8

For the beginner, this is most easily accomplished by dedicating the instrument, member by member, to the work of the Soul. He gives his hands to the Soul, relinquishing all right of control of them to his higher consciousness. He then observes the resulting activity. He then gives his eyes, his ears, his organs of speech, etc., until he has dedicated his entire instrument to the Soul.

After a consideration of this four-fold vibratory activity, the aspirant has a glimpse of the type and quality of influence he exerts upon his environment. The obvious disciplinary measures are taken, and gradually he learns to control his vibratory impact upon others. He applies every concept of Truth which he has grasped to the task of daily living, and thus brings his affairs into Intelligent Activity.

The Path of Initiation

INDEX TO THE PATH OF INITIATION

Index

Index

Index

Index

The Path of Initiation

Further Information

For further information on *Ashramic Projections*, and related courses and materials, see:

www.wisdomimpressions.com

or write to us at:

WisImp@wisdomimpressions.com

or

Wisdom Impressions
P.O. Box 6457
Whittier, CA 90609–6457